Livery Kirkby Fields

Kate Higgins

For Mum and Dad

"The Lord watch between me and thee;When we are absent one from another"

The bells ring out at Christmas
To every Christian heart,
To invite us in their ringing
When we are far apart.

With Best Wishes
for a Merry Christmas and
a Happy New Year.

To Madge
from Ted.

(1950)

Chapters

Chapter One

Mornings

"Julie - Gerry - Eddie - Kathy - Margaret - John -
Monica, Sheila!.......
Rise and shine!"

That was mum's roll call and our cue to get up,
which I heard from under the bedclothes. It's a
freezing cold January day so this is where I'm staying
for a while. I woke up shivering in the night,
reaching for my big fat eiderdown but when I looked
over the edge of my bed I saw it lying on the floor,
again. It's always slipping from under my bedspread.
I tried tucking the blankets between the mattress and
the wall to try to keep myself warm but it didn't
work and I couldn't reach to pick the eiderdown up
from the top bunk without getting out of bed.

Work or school days in our house start pretty much
the same, come rain, hail or shine. At half past
seven, as regular as clockwork, we can rely on mum
to take a few seconds out of the kitchen to wake us,
calling from the bottom of the stairs. We don't need
an alarm clock, all apart from dad that is, who tells
me he has two, one he keeps on a table next to the
bed and one on the other side of the room, in a
biscuit tin. He tells me the one in the tin bangs and
clatters enough to wake the dead and I tell him I'll
have to take his word for that because I've never
heard any of his clocks, they've certainly never
woken me, not at the ungodly hour he gets up. I

really don't know what the world looks like at that time and would prefer it to stay that way.

I'm not sure how or when mum wakes up, come to think of it. She does get to bed of course but I feel somehow that it isn't for very long because she's up so late doing her jobs, jobs and more endless jobs. Mum says she's a born worrier and that doesn't make for good sleeping when she does try but you'll never hear her complain as she spends her days plodding systematically through whatever needs doing.

The ear piercing wail I hear now is our reminder call. It isn't mum having gone over the edge like she's always saying she will. She says we'll see her in Rainhill yet, the local psychiatric hospital. We were driving past the building a while ago when she said, "There it is, that's where you'll be coming to see me", but she's joking of course. She's made it this far after all. The sound is the siren from the BICC cable factory, a fifteen minute walk away in the next town of Melling, warning the staff they have ten minutes to get to work. This is what we call the "ten to eight horn" and it serves us as well as the factory staff. In fact Julie gets out of bed the minute the horn goes off every work day and she's just gone into the bathroom now. Clocks or no clocks, you can't really oversleep when you live in a house with nine other people. I should know, the amount of times I tried to get out of going to school by pretending to be asleep. I'd lie still with my eyes closed while havoc wreaked around me, in the hope that mum would think it was a shame to wake me because I must be so tired. It never worked though, mum would gently call me until I had to open my eyes. I went on to find a trick that did work, several times, but I can't say what I did as that would be telling and besides, judging by the looks I have been given by those few I have told, in retrospect I think it was perhaps a bit stupid.

Drawing by Harry – aged 7

Dad's at work already and mum is back in the kitchen, singing as she does most days. Gerry and Eddie have also left for work, having had their breakfast of porridge out of the huge pan mum will have stirred for ten minutes, followed by toast, all eaten in the warmth of the kitchen which is heated by the coal burning stove in the corner of the room, spreading it's heat to the hallway but not much further. The scrubbed pine kitchen table will be set with an assortment of mismatched crockery and cutlery and whatever is left of the toasted sliced loaf will be on the table. The table, as well as a matching pine dresser, came from mum's parents' house. Mum's mother died about nine years before I was born and her father died when I was a baby so I didn't know either of my maternal grandparents. From the tales mum tells of her childhood, it is clear that she knew better days, which she likes to reminisce about, while I like to listen.

There are usually just about enough every day cups and saucers to go round as they are always being dropped and broken, but we never did have to resort to drinking out of the jam jars like we used to joke about in days gone by. Thank goodness, it never came to that. The financial strain is starting to ease a bit now for mum and dad now that the eldest of us are working and contributing to our keep and mum even has a full china tea set in the display cabinet in the front room, kept for best and for visitors, both the china and the front room, that is.

We live in the back room which we used just as the dining room until recently as Mum and dad are starting to get the downstairs nice now. They decorated the front room with blue wallpaper embossed with very faint white vertical lines and we now have our first ever fitted carpet, in blue. It is beautiful. Up until now we have always had wall to wall lino with a rug over it but lino wears into holes quickly as it gets walked over so much, especially with the amount of traffic in our house. Dad has boxed in the old coal fireplace and tiled fire surround, with hardboard painted to look like wood and we have a two bar electric fire in place of the old coal fire. It's all nice and clean looking and we don't have to empty the grate in the mornings any more but the electric fire doesn't throw any heat out so you have to practically sit on it to get warm. It looks good though and quite posh, which isn't a word I ever thought I'd use about our house, but I won't get carried away because I haven't finished talking about upstairs yet.

Heat may rise, but not much reaches up here in these temperatures, in fact it's getting colder by the minute so I'm going deeper under the covers. On some winter nights and at weekends we have a paraffin heater in the bathroom which isn't worth using in the mornings as it takes so long to heat up, at least an hour before it takes the chill off the room. After a couple of hours the room can get quite warm but by this time the paraffin will have burned away so it is only a short term measure for keeping the freeze off. The smell of the paraffin is enough to knock you out but at the same time it is comforting because you know when you smell the fumes the temperature will be above freezing point.

I suppose I could ask Margaret, who is in the bottom bunk, to pass my eiderdown to me but I don't want to disturb her. It's not that I'm all that kind, it's because I want to get to the bathroom before she does when Julie comes out, so I'd rather Margaret stays comfortable where she is.

John, Monica and Sheila are around somewhere, getting ready for school, so that leaves just me and Margaret left in bed. While I'm waiting for my turn in the bathroom I lie and muse like I do most mornings, dreaming of better times to come when I will wake up in a bedroom of my choice, not this tip. I'm not dropping my guard on the bathroom door though and am listening for Julie coming out, ready for the daily battle to commence between me and Margaret. This rigmarole over the bathroom will really have to stop because as Monica pointed out to me the other day, one of the hinges is working loose on the door from where we've been banging it and there'll be hell to pay from dad if it comes off its hinge altogether.

Margaret beat me. Actually she does most days as she can make a faster dart from the bottom bunk, but she'd better not start running that bath or the door won't be the only thing in danger of becoming unhinged.

I've now braved the cold and emerged from under the covers to face the day and as I lie here looking at the sheen on the wallpaper I half close my eyes again. It's not that I'm drifting off, there's fat chance of that with the noise going on around here. The toilet sounds like a fog horn whenever we pull the chain which dad tells us off for when he hears it, as he says there's no need to play "God Save Ireland" every time we go to the toilet. We used to laugh at this, not having any idea what he was on about until one day he gave us a demonstration by standing by the toilet and giving the chain one firm pull which flushed first time. He then showed us how not to do it, the way we all did, by standing to attention and pulling on the chain in short bursts while singing:-

"God save Ireland, said the heroes
God save Ireland, said they all
Whether on the scaffold high
Or the battlefield we die
Oh, what matters when for Erin dear we fall"

The demo didn't change anything, as it would seem that dad is the only one with the knack. Meanwhile, back to the morning story where John is drumming in time with the radio which is blaring away and mum is now singing April Love, to her own tune. No, I'm just trying to make the wallpaper look better by blinking against the glare of the light bulb.

I feel that I should say here that if I had been telling this story yesterday then it wouldn't have been quite the same - as yesterday was my birthday. I'm seventeen. Margaret let me go into the bathroom first but before that and after Julie had gone in, she called up to me telling me she had my present. She kept that well hidden. It was such a lovely present too, which must have cost half a week's wages - a bottle of Helena Rubenstein's Apple Blossom perfume.

As I reached out for the nearest place to put down my perfume, my hand rested on Julie's dressing table as the familiar feeling of guilt crept up on me. Julie, as the eldest, had more responsibility than mum and dad would have liked while she was growing up and when she was eighteen and the rest of us were old enough to help with the chores, she wasn't allowed to do any real work around the house. Then mum and dad bought her her own bedroom suite comprising of a wardrobe, dressing table with three mirrors and a chest of drawers. A bedroom suite might have been commonplace in your average household but this furniture would be the nicest possession Julie had ever had. Then one day while she was at work and I was experimenting with her make up, I spilled nail varnish remover all over the dressing table top, removing half the surface. Everyone was so angry with me but they don't know how sorry I was and still am. Mum and dad did have the dressing table re-varnished but it isn't quite the same and I haven't done myself any favours with Julie who has taken to locking her nice things away.

Before I left for work yesterday I popped into the front room to see if dad had left my birthday half crown on the mantelpiece. He had remembered. I wasn't sure I still qualified now that I'm working but there it was. I went to Littlewoods in Church Street for lunch with my friend, Sharon from work. For one and six I bought steak and kidney pie and chips, a cup of tea and apple pie with custard.

Mum had given me a green tartan patterned shoulder bag which I would like if it wasn't for the fact that Trudie, one of the women at work, has one exactly the same and Sharon laughs at it. Having said that, we both laugh at most of what Trudie says or does, so maybe the bag will be alright. Her office is at the end of the corridor at work and every day at lunch time we hear her shake a load of tablets out onto her desk. I don't know how many she takes but she must rattle. Mum bought my bag from T J Hughes in London Road in town. I know this because it's been sitting in a TJ's carrier bag for a week.

Sharon is one of my "rich" friends. She lives in Allerton, a leafy part of Liverpool and she is the only child of a policeman, a "Chief Inspector", as she keeps telling me, and they live in a palace. It's a show house and couldn't be any more different than ours. When I first met Sharon and we chatted about our families, she seemed fascinated with my tales of home. At first I thought she was making fun of the way we lived and I clammed up but then I realised that she was genuinely interested and strangely enough, even seemed envious of the fun we had. She now asks me for stories every day and we laugh together.

I went round to Sharon's house once for tea. We had three fish fingers each with a slice of bread and butter and some peas. Her mum, who works in Lewis's, spent the whole of the short time we ate our tea, wiping round the kitchen after cooking and telling Sharon she had to lose weight, while I was too thin. I thought this sounded promising and hoped it might mean I would get a bit more to eat, maybe a piece of home made cake or something else that wouldn't mess the kitchen up. I had no such luck, there was no sign of the baking always evident at home, not even a crumb that I could see on the floor, which was carpeted by the way, with big thick grey tiles that reminded me of horsehair. I've never seen anything like that in my life and had to laugh when I imagined having carpet in our kitchen at home, trying to clean off the stew or porridge stains. Suitably unimpressed, I left with Sharon as we headed off to Wimpey's in town for a burger.

Sharon's family have recently moved into their show house and Sharon told me after my teatime visit that her mum said they would soon be decorating the spare room and would be buying a white carpet for it and I would be able to stay over. My first thought was how to get out of that one. They have fitted carpets all through the house, luxuriously thick ones at that. No rugs on lino there. I would love mum to have a house like that but some things are not meant to be and I know a posh house isn't all there is to life. I don't think I'll be staying there overnight though, white carpet or not, I'd be too scared to move in case I damaged anything, so will make my excuses if ever I am asked. It hasn't been mentioned since so maybe they are still looking for a thick enough carpet.

I don't see how I could invite Sharon to our house but she's never asked so far. If she ever does I'll make excuses. I suppose while I'm willing to traipse all the way to hers she's happy not to put herself out by coming to see me. It's a shame really because I would like to be free and easy and not to have to act like I have something to hide, but it's one thing laughing with Sharon about the fun we have at home and quite another thing to expect that she could actually have any concept of the cramped conditions we live in. I don't want the embarrassment of that, hers or mine, so this way I don't have to answer the inevitable questions about how we all fit in and where we all sleep etc.

The dimensions of our front room are 10 ft x 16 ft including the bay, which gives us a bit less than 160 square feet in total. This means if we were all to stand in the room together we would have just over one and a half square yards each. That doesn't sound too bad but the living room at the back where we spend most of our time now, only gives us one square yard each.

I'm looking now at the condensation on the bedroom wall which through half closed eyes could be wallpaper with a glossy sheen, over a green leafy pattern but I'm a dreamer and in my dreams the room can look any way I want it to, be it a gypsy caravan to a pop star mansion and I can change it as often as I like.

The wallpaper would have been chosen and put up by Mr and Mrs O'Mara, our predecessors, during their time in the house. I helped dad paint over two of the walls a while ago to cover the damp stains, that's the window wall and the one opposite. We used Walpamur emulsion in a light creamy colour with paint left over from when dad painted the top half of the hall but as we were running out of paint, we watered it down to finish the one wall which is now translucent and the pattern shows through. The paint hasn't done a lot for the stains actually. I was thinking of asking dad if we could run to some more paint but wonder, as I close my eyes again, if it's worth the bother. It always looks a bit of a mess in here anyway, no matter how hard mum tries to make it nice and it's not as if anyone outside the family ever sees the room so, it only matters to us.

Our sleeping arrangements have varied over the years but currently we have our bunk beds on one side of the chimney breast with Julie on the other side and her dressing table just about fits in between, covering up an ugly, brown tiled fireplace. Monica and Sheila share a "three quarter" size bed, acquired through what we thought of at the time as a rare act of kindness from Mrs O'Mara who we used to live next door to. I'm not so sure now how kind that was as the more I thought about it, the more I realised that she most likely wanted rid of the bed anyway and we did her a favour by graciously accepting it. It was equally rare for mum and dad to accept any form of charity.

The acquisition of the bed came about when the council embarked on a project of upgrading the interior of the houses which involved moving the occupants of each house along to the house next door, while their own was worked on. This house is on the end of a row and although it has the same amount of rooms, the dimensions are considerably bigger than next door and as every square foot counts, when we moved in from next door for the renovations, we stayed here, along with the bed. Mr and Mrs O'Mara moved into one of the flats on the estate. Mr O'Mara was always pleasant and would smile and say hello but I think his wife got a bit fed up of the noise we made, for which I can't say I blame her really as we all get fed up with it. Every so often she would ask mum to keep us quiet in the mornings, especially at weekends as her daughter, "My Mary", needed a lie in after a hard week working in the tax office.

When we lived next door, I shared a double bed with one or two of my sisters, the bed being placed alongside the coal fireplace, again a brown tiled one. Although it was too dangerous to have a fire in the bedroom generally, very occasionally, around Christmas time or if one of us was ill, like the time Margaret, Monica and I had measles, then dad would light a coal fire. Anyone who hasn't slept in a Victorian bed, on a sprung mattress two feet deep, under the weight of heavy blankets and an eiderdown or two, while watching the flames of a coal fire dance around the room, simply does not know what they have missed. With three of us in the bed, any blanket shortage could be overcome by the use of old coats.

I have a last look around the room before getting out of bed now that the bathroom is free. As I walk towards the door I look up at the two windows which floodlight the room on summer mornings, but of course it's still dark now so we have the light on. Nothing matches and the beds are covered with an assortment of candlewick bedspreads. There's a pink one on the big bed and a variety of colours over the eiderdowns on the others.

Between them mum and dad provide us with the food on the table and the security of a home it's good to come back to. We live in a three bedroomed, one bathroomed terraced house with gardens to the front and rear. In the back garden we have two apple trees and one pear tree. Dad likes the garden and I know he would like to spend more time working in it if he could. He does sometimes manage a few summer flowers such as forget me nots, which he seems to like, or nasturtiums which grow like wildfire. Julie is quite green fingered and will plant flowers occasionally so some years the garden is colourful. I love all flowers and would love to see roses in our garden, but there have not been any roses so far.

Sefton Close 1942

Sefton Close 2012

Not much gets wasted round here. We even found clay to play with in the garden when we were little which was good enough to mould little bowls and cups to play house with. Also in our old garden, which of course is next door now, if anybody ever digs it up, can be found the "treasure" we buried of a few old coins, possibly including a farthing or two and other such things we thought people in the future might be interested in finding. We would start off by trying to dig to Australia but our enthusiasm always waned when we saw no change after digging a couple of feet deep. I would only be about four at the time.

The back garden led off from the door to the "back kitchen" next door. I don't know why we called it the back kitchen as it isn't as if we had more than one. Mum used to line jam jars filled with water along the outside window sill, every day in the summer, leaving a bit of jam inside to attract and trap the wasps in the jars. I could never understand the reason for that as it meant we had to dodge the wasps whenever we went in and out of the door and there was many a time I was too scared to go inside when they were buzzing around. In fact I don't ever remember seeing a wasp trapped in a jar, they just ate the jam. We have a side door to this house and have to walk round to the garden so at least wasps around the door is something I no longer need to worry about.

I was fourteen the day we moved in from next door. We were all excited at the change which felt like exploring another house when you go on holiday. As I happily collected all my things together I picked up one of the cardboard packing boxes and it was then that I realised that everything I owned, including my clothes, all fitted into the one small box. When things were spread around and not needed at the same time, I never noticed just how little there was. Seeing the true picture of my possessions that day brought home to me just how little we had beyond the bare necessities and it made me think of my best friend from school, Linda, and of how lucky she was.

We all like nice things but we can live without them and I found the hardest part was trying to keep from other people the material things we lacked. Linda has just the one sister and always talked a lot about all her clothes while I kept my mouth shut. She once told me how she went shopping with her mum every Saturday and was bought something new to wear every week. Her mum thought she went along to keep her company when it was really just for what she would buy her. I couldn't understand how she could treat her mum like that. I would never say I was envious - envy is pointless but I did of course wish that some things were different. I never told Linda or anybody else for that matter about my thoughts on moving day; there are some things you learn to keep quiet about if you want to keep your pride. Something else I never told Linda either, was how I thought her pretty clothes would look much better on me but then I'm sure she wouldn't have agreed with me.

You could say we are still quite poor compared to our peers and our neighbours and we feel it, but we wouldn't be half as bothered if it didn't seem to matter to other people so much. Had we been around fifty or so years earlier then we might have walked barefoot to school, as would our neighbours, but some of them seem to have amazingly short or selective memories and act as if they have always lived in the Land of Plenty. We have always been well fed and warm, better fed than some of my friends from my school days in some cases it seemed, as when we would ask each other what we had had for tea the night before and we'd had say, pork chops, if it had been a Tuesday, they would look surprised and say they never had pork chops because they were too dear. One of these girls once told me that her parents went abroad on holiday while she stayed with her granny. A foreign holiday is expensive so I suppose there wouldn't be much to spare to buy pork chops.

Like most families, we have the same menu for tea for each night of the week but where others might have cold meat left over from their Sunday joint on a Monday, we don't have any left over so our Monday tea is egg, chips and peas with bread and butter and a pot of tea. Mum is a really good cook - I've never known her to spoil anything. I love chips, of course, and am sure our Monday tea of chips dipped in runny egg is much nicer than cold meat. Margaret likes tomatoes and no matter what we have for tea she gets up from the table to get a tomato and every night as we sit down Gerry asks her, "What's te marter with you?" Roast chicken is my favourite dinner, but this is mainly reserved for Easter as poultry is so expensive and we have to buy two, to go round. I am looking forward to the day I can have a chicken leg but as I'm sixth in line for this privilege in our house, I'll most likely have to wait until I'm married.

Back to Monday night's tea. The teapot and cups

will be set on the table and tea is usually late because mum has to finish the washing. Tuesday will vary between either pork or lamb chops, braising steak or stew, or scouse as some people call it but we're not allowed to as mum says its common. You can tell as soon as you walk through the door, and catch sight of the kitchen when it's stew for tea, because the pan of meat will have been on the stove for about four hours with the boiling stock evaporating and dripping down the walls. The way mum cooks braising steak is perfect. She cooks it on a high gas, number 7, for 30 minutes then two hours at number 3. She makes the gravy by sprinkling Burdall's gravy salt into a mixture of flour and water, with the water being added until the consistency is just right. If anyone happens to be passing by whilst this delicate operation is being performed, they're quite likely to be asked by mum to pass her a cup of water as she stands by the stove with such a look of deep concentration that you'd think she was performing surgery but mum always has that expression when she's concentrating. Wednesday tea is one of Tuesday's alternatives and Thursday is fish and chip night from the chip shop. Friday is home cooked fish with chips if the fish is fried, or mashed potato if it is the yellow fish which mum calls "finnan haddie" or smoked haddock, which I think must be an acquired taste because some people seem to like it. The Friday fish is of course, because as Catholics we don't eat meat on Fridays. On Saturdays we usually have a quick tea of something with chips, such as Cornish pasty or ham, because we eat at different times as people get ready to go out. Saturday is the one night of the week that we don't sit down together to eat. The Saturday menu may be a general thing as one of my friends Ann, says she likes Saturday night tea in their house because everyone has something different and she has a bit of everything.

Our home lives could perhaps be best described as organised chaos with mum and dad as the organisers while we provide the chaos. We all get on pretty well together for the most part. Gerry and Eddie are best mates and John who is five years younger than Eddie strives to be one of their gang. The only real squabbling you'll hear is between me and Margaret as we fight all the time, not just over the bathroom but over everything. The problem as I see it is the age gap as there are just thirteen months between us and we have always been treated the same, never seeming to have had any individuality as even the neighbours and our aunties get our names mixed up. Perhaps it would have been better if we'd been born twins when maybe we could have been happy to be the same. I'm not sure that mum would agree, as she gives up on us. One of her often heard sayings is, "The older you get, the worse you get".

Mum has a lot of regular sayings, one for most occasions but the one she uses just when things are going so wrong that they can't get much worse and then they do, is "I'm well blessed aren't I?" This will be used such times as when she sent one of us (who shall remain nameless) to Roberts' shop in Melling for a few groceries, with a five pound note and the money was lost, never to be seen again by the time that person was across the road with the door barely shut behind them. That was a big chunk of dad's week's wages gone and he had a bit more to say than mum did when he found out. That most definitely was not one of our better days.

Julie's getting married to her John in October and us four girls are to be bridesmaids. John says he was first introduced to Julie as he was passing by our house one day and dad looked up as he was polishing a shelf. When he saw John he said, "I've got five daughters, can you take one of them off my hands?", so John duly obliged. We are under strict instructions from Julie to behave in church as if anyone giggles during the ceremony she said she'll turn round and give them a belt. Each time we've been for fittings it's ended in laughter so I can understand her concern. The dresses Julie has chosen are all lovely. Ours are midnight blue while hers is the traditional white dress and veil which contrasts beautifully with her jet black hair.

Julie aged 3

Although we are similar to look at in a lot of ways, we all have different hair and eye colourings. Julie has straight, black hair and green eyes; Gerry's hair is a curly reddish brown and he has brown eyes; Eddie has the black hair and vivid blue eyes like dad; my hair is dark but not black, and isn't straight like I would prefer, and my eyes are blue; Margaret's hair is a chestnut colour and more curly than mine - she has green eyes; John has the black hair and blue eyes like Eddie and dad; Monica has the same straight jet black hair as Julie, with hazel eyes like mum and Sheila has mid brown hair and brown eyes.

Gerry is perhaps the most sensitive of my three brothers and also the funniest. Sometimes he doesn't even have to say anything as the expression on his face will speak for itself. He can even make you laugh on a Monday morning when you don't want to go to work. We listen to Tony Blackburn on Radio 1 in the mornings but I think Gerry could do his job better. He scared me for a minute the other night though while we were watching television. I could see something pink on the floor behind the television that looked like cotton wool covered in blood. I'd been looking at it dubiously for some time and eventually I asked Gerry if he knew what it was. With a straight face he said, "I think it's a throat", got up, picked it up and through it at me. I screamed and he laughed. It turned out to be a ball the dog had been pulling at and the pink bits were the stuffing.

Yes, we have a dog as well - he's called Rover and we inherited him from Uncle Mick, (dad's brother) who remarried a couple of years ago and his dog was not part of the marriage package. Uncle Mick has always been a practising Catholic and divorced his wife many years after she deserted him and their two daughters. Apparently Uncle Mick had originally wanted the divorce to protect his daughters' inheritance, "If anything happened to him", and then some years later he did meet and marry his second wife, Isabel. He applied for dispensation from the Pope to re-marry in church but was refused and so he had to marry in a registry office which I don't think was fair because he was the innocent party and had done so well for his girls.

Gerry once taught me what could become a very valuable lesson which unfortunately came too late for the time I spoiled Julie's dressing table, but is something I will try to bear in mind for the future. His words of wisdom came one day when he caught me messing around with his record collection and he said, "Don't touch what you can't afford". I'd been looking to see if he had anything more up to date than Johnny Cash but he didn't.

Eddie now, who unlike Gerry who is quite shy, is the most genial and outgoing of all of us and he seems to know everybody from miles around. You only have to mention a name and Eddie will assure you he has met that person and knows all about them. He gets it right as well more often than not. Mum says he's always been like that and ever since he could first talk he would chat away to anyone they came across in shops, buses etc. He's always bringing things home that he's found lying on the ground - sometimes good stuff and at others, things that "might come in handy". Mum says he must walk along with his head down watching the ground. I think I can sum Eddie up by saying he is interested in everybody and everything and a firm believer that for everything there is a purpose.

I'm next and then comes Margaret, another chatterbox. Dad says someone winds her up every morning and it takes all day for her to wind down again. He once asked me to find Margaret as he needed to talk to her and he said, "You'll find her looking in a mirror somewhere". I wish I had her confidence. Margaret really does like nice things and I think she's a bit of a dreamer like me. Recently mum was doing a run through of her hopes and fears for us all and when it came to Margaret she said she had no worries about Margaret, she could take care of herself but the day she would worry would be when she walks in with a driving licence.

Then there's John. I overheard dad saying recently how he regrets not having had as much time to spend with Gerry and Eddie while they were growing up as he would have liked and I think he tries to make up for lost time with John. Like Eddie and Margaret, John is more outgoing than the rest of us and very funny.

He's in the fourth year at St Bede's school in Ormskirk now and tells us how, when he first started in the second year, they had a new form teacher who took a register of the full names of the whole class. John listened while almost every other child announced their two Christian names, and having just the one name, he decided to make one up so when asked he gave his two first names as John Reginald. The teacher believed him and now all his school reports bear that name. When mum first saw the name "Reginald" on his report she was about to get on to the school, not very happy that they couldn't get his name right but luckily we stopped her in time.

John is always, as he puts it "trading" things with his school friends. He came home one day with a very expensive looking fountain pen and a pocket full of other treasures he said he'd exchanged with one boy for a rare penny. Any boy that John thinks he can get the better of he describes as having "A skinny head, buck teeth and glasses." It didn't work on that occasion though as the penny was just an ordinary one he'd taken out of his pocket and he didn't know that the boy's dad was a policeman and not so easily taken in as his son - so John had to return the goods.

John is quite inventive and when we were a bit younger he would come into our room at bed time to tell us "Mrs O'Mara and Johnny" stories. When Mrs O'Mara complained about the noise we made in the mornings and also occasionally blamed John for things he hadn't done, our line of defence was to make up these stories, or rather John did with our encouragement. I suspect John was inspired by Dennis the Menace in "The Beano". Admittedly, when a ball was accidentally thrown through a neighbour's window John would sometimes be responsible but certainly not always and he spent many an hour and many a week's pocket money during school holidays replacing neighbours' windows. The injustice came about whenever there was a broken window in the vicinity and we would hear calls of, "Where's that Johnny?"

And so this gave rise to his imaginary stories when we could lose ourselves in scenes of his escapades involving our former neighbour. A favourite tale was of Johnny watching for Mrs O'Mara to leave her house to go into town, leaving the house empty for several hours. Before she left the house, Johnny would have watched her through her back kitchen window as she baked a cake, dripping with chocolate, for tea. She would leave the cake on the kitchen table to cool while she was out shopping. As soon as the coast was clear Johnny would climb through the kitchen window which was never quite closed completely, and help himself to a piece of cake before climbing back out of the window.

Another favourite was Johnny watching Mrs O'Mara, again through the kitchen window, as she spring cleaned the house before going shopping, having washed the kitchen floor last of all. We could picture the whole house gleaming and spic and span. Johnny would again climb through the window and pick up Mrs O'Mara's coal scuttle to carry through the house, scattering the contents as he walked through. The scenes always ended in Mrs O'Mara arriving home with Johnny watching through the window as she screamed, "Where's that Johnny?!" Oh how we laughed.

None of us had seen Mrs O'Mara's kitchen either through the window or otherwise and I pictured it in the stories as exactly the same as ours, but of course I saw that it was different when we moved into her house.

I'll move on now to Monica who strangely enough, I think I have the most in common with and we spend a lot of time together now we are older. I say strange because Monica is very good, well behaved at all times and almost always does as she is told. Quite the opposite to me really but we laugh at the same things and have similar interests. I don't love anyone any more or any less, it's just that we get on well.

I'm ready to leave for work now and I'm hoping I can dodge mum and get away without having to eat any breakfast because ever since I started work I can't eat in the mornings. Mum doesn't seem to understand and thinks it's just because I'm rushing and unless I can escape it, she stands at the door with a cup of milk which she forces me to drink before I leave and then I feel sick all the way to work on the train. As I never leave the house without a goodbye kiss from mum, dodging some sustenance isn't easily possible. I wish I could eat breakfast as some days I feel faint and have actually passed out several times on buses or trains and most often, horror of horrors, in church, where I once found myself coming round while being carried out by two men. My first thought as I was coming round was to reach and pull up my coat and skirt to cover my dignity. I could have died of embarrassment.

And so, another day is launched as Margaret and I leg it to the station to catch the train to Exchange Station in Liverpool, a journey which takes around fifteen minutes on the Bury to Liverpool line. The two carriages are practically full before the train arrives at Kirkby so we have to stand most days in the guard's van when the seats are all taken. We travel with a group of other girls all working in offices in the city centre so I actually like the guard's van because we all get to stand together to chat and catch up on gossip but it does get very stuffy in there sometimes. It can be worse in the winter with the heating and the smell of diesel and like I said, I find it difficult to eat first thing in the mornings and if mum makes me drink milk I feel nauseous on the train. Another drawback is that the motion of the train, combined with my feeling queasy can set off the dizziness and make me feel faint.

We've been on the train for ten minutes now and it's starting again. I don't believe it and start to wonder, "Why, oh why didn't I find a seat"? It's too late now. I can hear the familiar buzzing and realise that I'm going to pass out if I don't sit down soon. I can't see Margaret but one of the girls is talking to me. She can't see that I'm trying to tell her what's happening, probably because my mouth isn't actually moving, as she carries on talking. The effort is too much and I give in to the blackness that now surrounds me.

I can hear people talking. The voices sound distant but are getting closer as my consciousness returns. I still feel a long way away and am reluctant to open my eyes. I feel very comfortable and sleepy and know there will be a sea of concerned looking faces staring down at me and I also know I will be very, very embarrassed when I wake up fully.

Eventually I half open my eyes to squint at the wintry sun which is now flooding through the window of the guard's van. I can see the outlines of the people in silhouette but they all look black in the sunlight. I'm going to have to get up and know it's too much to expect people not to be fussing. So here goes. Maybe one day I'll learn how to stop embarrassing myself.

Chapter Two

The Walk

I'm blinded by the sunlight streaming through the trees as I shield my eyes to see the outline of the station building, as I cross Glover's Brow. Turning round I can see clearly the ground where the station used to be.

It is over 30 years since I last made that journey to town and since I last heard mum's roll call as it's 25 years since she died and I stopped visiting Kirkby regularly. I do visit occasionally and last walked through the estate a couple of years ago with Monica, our children and my two little grandsons, pointing out some of the landmarks of our childhood. We also called on Mr and Mrs Bolton, the parents of my best friend, Pauline, when we were children. We were attending a christening party at the time, being held at Waverley House, on South Park Road.

Waverley House, now a listed building, is known to the people of Kirkby both past and present as the big old house, clearly visible from the trains and the roads passing through Kirkby, and has served as the premises of the local Conservative Club since the 1960s. It is a building that never changes in any way and it's good to see it looking the same as ever - just as dismal and creepy as it ever was. The grounds are devoid of flowers, with not so much as a daisy to be seen, and an inspiration to any imaginative child surrounded by concrete, with a mind open to the suggestion that there is more to life than meets the eye. I spent many a happy hour here when I was growing up, gazing at the many windows of the three storey building, right up to the tower, willing a ghost to appear, but it never did.

Waverley House 2012 - Timeless

I'm walking round the estate again today, on my own at first while waiting to meet Monica, but with a different purpose this time. As a child I was the inquisitive one, always asking questions and I'm still reminded by my siblings of how well mum and dad named me, after "Keyhole Kate" from the Dandy comic. Any physical resemblance I bore to the skinny, bespectacled character was enhanced by the round, pink National Health glasses I first wore when I was ten.

The question I am asking today is one that I never asked mum and as it's too late to ask her now, looking back on my childhood as an adult might give me the answer I would like.

My question is, "How could you sing mum, with all you had on your plate? I don't remember a time since I was about 3 or 4 years old that I wasn't aware of the hardships you and dad lived through. Not that the difficulties were pressed home - they didn't need to be; we saw them first hand."

Turning left from Glover's Brow into Kirkby Row I can see where the original Kirkby Post Office building once stood, about two hundred yards down on the left hand side of the road with nothing in between that building and St Chad's church apart from the fields. This was where we first called to collect mum's Family Allowance and to be interrogated by Sally, the Post Mistress, for snippets of gossip. Sally was a tiny woman about the same height as me when I was ten. I first noticed her height the day mum sent me to take some clothes to the dry cleaners and I saw Sally coming towards me as I was on my way back home. She walked straight up to me, looked into the then empty shopping bag I was carrying and asked me if I had been shopping. Some of the words I'd heard dad use came to mind as she approached, because I knew I was in for a grilling, it was written all over her face which lit up as she quickened her pace when she saw me. I couldn't so very well tell her to "bugger off" so I just said "Yes". She looked again into the bag, saying how I hadn't bought much and that's when I saw that we were the same height. She wouldn't have dared to ask mum such questions but I would have loved to have seen her try - she would have walked away with a flea in her ear and feeling her height then. Mum was nobody's fool.

Sally wasn't the only one of the neighbours to pry into our business. Over the years we became used to people taking advantage of the fact that we couldn't answer back. They asked questions they wouldn't ask mum and certainly not dad, so we found our own ways of dealing with them. I didn't have a problem seeing through people but knowing how to handle unkind comments wasn't easy. I never felt in any way inferior but did grow up feeling I had to prove that I wasn't. One of the neighbours once went so far as to ask me if we had enough to eat in our house because we were all so thin. It didn't help our case that we were all, as dad put it, "like long streaks of bacon", just like him. We were brought up being told it was rude to eat in the street but I took that comment to heart so much that I followed it up by slipping out of the house one day with a couple of home made buttered scones and walking up and down the road as I ate them, just to prove that we did get fed. I would only be about eight at the time and got a telling off from mum when she found out as she asked me what I was thinking of, walking down the road eating. I said I was sorry and wouldn't do it again but never told her my reason.

The following pictures were taken by David Long, a neighbour from the estate, along with his message:-

"I took them from the tower of St Chad's - I climbed out onto the outside ledges practically all the way round. I must have been mad....

They start from looking almost East - the water tower on School Lane/ County Road, modelled, we were told, on the keep of Warwick Castle, is in the centre, with St Greg's RC Comp to the right, with the new Melling Drive estate centre in the foreground.

Then a bit further round, with the estate beyond the Vicarage Glebe Field and the extension to the graveyard. St Greg's is to the left, and Ruffwood Comp in the centre - I think the dark lump is a multi-storey going up.

The next has the roof of the Vicarage just visible, then some of St Chad's gardens, and then the town centre and Cherryfield Drive.

Then a swing further south, with the roundabout in front of Kirkby FE College before Valley Road was built."

School dominates the next one - with a start being made on the Poplar Drive estate to the right, and across the field. The railway is running from right to left behind the houses - leading up to Glovers Brow. The right-hand of the two white buildings beyond is, I think, the Carter's Arms - but I can't remember the other white building - the Sefton Close entrance to our estate was to one side or other of it.

Kirkby's first catholic church, Holy Angels, was built facing the site of Sally's Post Office. The original church has since been demolished and recently rebuilt on the same ground, now renamed as St Michael and All Angels.

We were in the parish of Most Holy Redeemer and St Kentigern, the pretty little old church, in Waddicar Lane, Melling which was known only to us as "Father Ramsbottom's" when we were children. Father Ramsbottom was a lovely man, always kind and considerate to mum. Whenever he called on us, unlike other houses he visited in the parish where he would collect any donation offered to the church as well as checking on the family's well-being, he only ever called on us to see that mum was OK and would never have expected a penny from her. One Easter Sunday as Julie, Gerry and Eddie were on their way out of mass, they were stopped by Father

43

Ramsbottom as he asked them to go and wait at his house just along the road, where he would meet them shortly. They went over and when he arrived he popped into the house to return with bags full of Easter eggs, one each for all of us. He said they were not to tell any of the other children in the parish but of course everyone knew by the time they arrived home. An Easter egg to us was a chocolate shell without any filling or frills and the only other one we had would be from mum and dad. Children didn't seem be given Easter eggs by aunties and uncles, grandparents, neighbours or indeed anybody who knew them, unlike today, at least not that I knew of, and as we would have more or less given chocolate up for Lent, our Easter eggs were a real treat.

Father Ramsbottom retired prematurely due to ill health and sent a lovely letter to mum before he left the parish. The church today no longer has its own priest but the parish is served by St Mary's chapel on Prescot Road in Aughton, by a mass being said there every Sunday morning. I called at St Kentigern's recently when it was closed up, but looking up through the windows I could just see the same two statues I saw as a child, one of Our Lady and one of the Sacred Heart, on either side of the altar. Father Ramsbottom would place tiny blue and silver coloured medals of Our Lady around the statue, attached to a piece of blue embroidery cotton, for the girls to take. Lots of those medals slipped through my fingers as a child, only to be lost or discarded but I found one amongst mum's personal belongings when she died, which is now kept with my treasured possessions.

Around the time Father Ramsbottom retired we started going to mass, the blessing service of benediction and confession, all at Holy Angels church where there were three priests and more of a choice of mass times, including one on Sunday evenings at half past six. One of the priests, Father Daniels, could put the fear of God into us on confession days. We went to confession every other Saturday afternoon as children when there would be two priests on duty. The normal process was to simply go into the confessional and confess to the usual sins of swearing, missing mass (if you were lucky), giving cheek to your mum or just made up sins if you couldn't think of any. For your penance you'd have to say three Hail Marys and make a good Act of Contrition (a prayer saying you're sorry). Father Daniels, however, would shout and bang on the door when he was ready for the next "confessor" while we sat outside quaking in our boots and trying to hang on to go to the other priest. Not that any priest could see who was on the other side of the dividing wall but you were always sure he would recognise your voice. I used to consider trying to disguise mine but didn't know how to, although I did wonder how many people have tried it to avoid being recognised. Outside confession Father Daniels was very chatty, young and good looking. He once asked me when I was fourteen, shortly after he had joined the parish, if I was Julie's sister. When I confirmed that I was, he said, "I thought so, I'd know those eyes anywhere." The remark made me feel uncomfortable and I never told anybody.

To my right now is Whitefield Drive, the route along which the number 92 bus took us to Liverpool city centre or to the stops en route, as well as my senior school of Notre Dame Collegiate in Everton Valley, the doctor's surgery which was just off Longmoor Lane in the next town of Fazakerley and the chemist's shop, (the chemist being the doctor's cousin, Mr Walters), the Rio cinema and the Co-op, all on Longmoor Lane. The 92 also took us to the shops in Walton Vale and the Astoria cinema on Walton Road. The Rio closed as a cinema and re-opened as a bingo hall during the 1960s. When mum and dad's financial burden started to ease, they began to enjoy the occasional night out and would visit the bingo hall. They won something on most of their visits as dad was quite lucky that way and there were treats for us all on those occasions.

Back to Whitefield Drive where just over half a mile down the road stands the Fantail pub. There is a bus stop outside the pub and when it was first opened the bus drivers started announcing the stop as "The Fantail", a name quickly adopted by the passengers. Long before the pub was built, however, the stop had been known as the "Pigeon House", after the building next to the pub which has stood since before buses were ever thought of.

The bus along Kirkby Row - 1960s

From the brief knowledge I had of the history of the Pigeon House, the small tower standing in front of Whitefield House, one of Kirkby's oldest houses, I knew it had originally been a dovecote. More recently I have looked into the origins of the building and discovered that it was built in 1703 and used as a pigeon cote at the top with the lower part used for keeping pigs. The building, along with Whitefield House, is now listed as an ancient monument by the English Heritage.

I was fascinated to learn that Whitefield House was used as a secret meeting place for recusants who remained catholic and refused to attend Anglican services, during the 18th century.

In 1770, Whitefield House was extended and some

time within the following few years, a young man by the name of Peter Beans attended the house for religious instruction in the Catholic faith. Peter, who was born at Pear Tree Farm, on Bewley Drive, (the site where St Gregory's girls' comprehensive school was subsequently built), at the age of 12, along with three other local brothers from the Glover family (the name since given to Glover's Brow), was sent to live in Hanover to further his theological studies.

Four years later the young men were forced by Napoleon's band of 30,000 to return to England. After firstly seeking refuge at a college in Yorkshire, Peter, whose name had since been changed to Baines, was ordained in the catholic faith into the Order of St Benedict. During the following twenty years he was to become ordained as a Bishop, and to become nationally recognised throughout both the Catholic and Anglican churches for his dignity and charm together with his eloquence as a preacher. In 1833 he returned to Liverpool to open St Anthony's Church on Scotland Road, around eighty years before my grandparents were married in the same church.

Kirkby is as steeped in history as anywhere else and the changes that took place happened so quickly and were so radical that the majority of us were not aware of Kirkby's history, apart from comprising of its few old farm houses. I now believe that researching the history of Kirkby would make a fascinating subject for anybody with such an interest, one or two books having already been written on the subject.

I turn left now into Glover's Brow to pass Sefton Cottage, the former home of the late Mr Frank Irlam and his family. Mr Irlam was one of the teachers at Kirkby's original village school. My knowledge of him was by reputation for being a very well respected teacher and member of society, although as a family we didn't know him personally.

Next is the site of the original railway ticket office where Mr McNamara, one of our neighbours from Mount Road on the estate was the stationmaster during the years I travelled on the line.

Across the road on the left is one of Kirkby's original beer only pubs, the Railway Hotel, another listed building, which looks just the same as ever from the outside. It was always a "man's" pub while I lived here which seemed to overflow on Sunday afternoons after the 11 o'clock mass at Holy Angels.

On the right hand side a bit further along still stands the newsagents, known in our time as "the top shop" and then next door a mini market has replaced the grocers' shop owned at the time by Mr and Mrs Campbell, another well respected couple who I recall liked to "give something back" to the community with their charitable works. One particular fund raising event they organised was the raffle of Mr Campbell's car. We were all lining up to buy tickets thinking there wouldn't be that many sold as the shop for the most part only served our estate and Westvale, so we'd be in with a fair chance. The owner of the winning ticket was due to be announced in the "Kirkby Reporter" and on the due day, the top shop had people queuing up for the paper before it had even arrived. It wasn't every day you had such a good chance of winning a car and everybody was excited as they scanned the pages only to see the winner announced as the Campbells' son. Any protests to Mr Campbell were met with being told that his son had as much right as anyone else to buy a ticket.

Both Mr and Mrs Campbell were sociable, outgoing people who looked after themselves well and would never be seen to let themselves go. However, I don't know how Mr Campbell expected people to react the day he decided to do something about his bald patch. After all, he was known and seen by the same people every day and it wasn't as if Julie and her friend Margaret wouldn't spot the difference the day they called at the shop on their way home from work one night to buy some ham for Margaret's lunch the following day. They were left standing with their mouths open when they looked up at Mr Campbell as he approached them and they saw that he was sporting a wig. They burst out laughing and had to leave the shop empty handed with Mr Campbell calling after them that they were barred. He got over it though and they did go back and he continued to wear the wig.

Next to Campbell's was a betting shop and amazingly, fifty years later, this row of shops remains, still used for much the same purposes with a betting shop still there. Dad liked a flutter on the horses and would sometimes send us to collect his winnings while he was at work. He also did the "Spot the ball" in the Liverpool Echo on a Saturday and once won a prize for getting a "near miss". There were celebrations and treats all round on that day.

Dad also did the pools every week and something which puzzled me over the years is why he never asked me to pick his numbers because as a child I had an unusual talent. Between the ages of about ten and twelve I picked the winning number on the television quiz show, "Take Your Pick" every week without fail. During the show, hosted by Michael Miles, the contestants chose one of ten boxes which held the key to opening a box numbered thirteen. When I closed my eyes I saw the number in my mind's eye, so I wish that dad had passed the pools coupon over to me.

This "psychic" power didn't last unfortunately but it was superseded after a gap of about ten years by my having the strange ability of knowing when somebody I associated with would be going away. As an example, in the workplace, I almost always would know when somebody was ready to hand in their notice. I was sitting at my desk one day when a colleague took one of many phone calls. As she picked up the receiver I knew that the call would be to offer her a job. She later told us that the call had been from a former employer who had asked her to return and she accepted the offer. At other times I would look at a person and know they were going to go. That all sounds very strange but it is true.

I once phoned a radio station for a reading from their guest medium, to be told I was "a bit of a witch". He said something about absorbing other people's energy, but I was so taken aback by being called a witch that unfortunately I couldn't take in the rest of what he said.

The Top Shop - 2012

The Post Office run by Sally eventually relocated into one of the shops at the end of this row, which was shared with the draper's shop where mum would buy the many yards of diamond patterned ribbon for our hair, in every colour imaginable. The shop also ran an agency for a dry cleaners which is where I had been on that day I met Sally.

The Carters Arms pub is across the road to the left which is another listed building. I haven't been inside the pub since I left Kirkby but it looks good from the outside and very well looked after and welcoming with a beer garden at the back.

The row of houses alongside the Carters Arms are named Inglehurst, Stanley Villa, Pemberton Villa and Homer Lea, respectively. These houses, more than any other of the buildings in Kirkby, held my fascination as a child. For a start they had a name rather than a number which set them apart immediately from our houses. Then the view from the roadside was obscured by overgrown trees and bushes which surrounded the houses, adding to their air of mystery. One house had a brick wall that was half in bits in the garden for years. To my mind, as a child, if somebody was rich enough to own one of these big houses with a name rather than a number, and then let the house get so run down, then they had to be eccentric. They had to be rich to be able to buy the house in the first place or - better still - it could be that the houses had been passed down from forebears whose portraits still hung on the walls and whose spirits stayed around to make sure nothing was changed. I pictured the insides of the houses to be wall to wall chintz and china. They would all have a piano and grandfather clock and cabbage would be boiling in the kitchen to be served up on china plates, with the family silver cutlery, like something from a scene in an old Margaret Rutherford film, with plenty of cats and bats thrown in for good measure. I used to look for the ghosts and whenever I passed by I would walk slowly in the hope of a sighting.

Today, the houses look quite ordinary from the

outside and don't hold the same mystery that they did when I was a child and they aren't that big either. The trees and bushes have gone, the paint isn't peeling from the windows and there are no crumbling walls surrounding the houses as they have all been removed. However, I still feel drawn to have a closer look to peep through the windows.

Inglehurst, Stanley Villa, Pemberton Villa and Homer Lea -2012

Just before continuing down Glover's Brow, I turn right at the crossroads into Mill Lane. The Tower Hill estate, the site of Kirkby's original water tower, was to be built at the end of the road, to the left of

County Road, some years later. Mill Lane never lost its country feel and whenever we walked down here or indeed continued down Glover's Brow on our way to a park in Melling where we used to play, we felt as if we were going into the country. Mill Lane is within the Kirkby boundary but some of the owners of the private houses built along here felt the need to tell people they lived in Melling rather than admit to living in Kirkby.

Continuing now, past the site of Woods' garage which served as a car mechanics as well as a petrol filling station. The garage building has now been converted into a house with new ones added on the site in place of the petrol tanks and other trappings of a garage. This was where the boys would buy odds and ends for their bikes and in fact one of the windows of the replacement house has a window in the same position where, according to Eddie, up until the garage closed not all that long ago, the same bits of bike were visible from the road, as were there when we were children. I'll take Eddie's word for that. A cable ran through the grounds of the garage and whenever a car rode over it a bell would alert the men working at the back that they had a customer. We never passed without standing on the cable and running away as one of the mechanics came out and although they were never quick enough to catch us, we must have been seen disappearing round the corner.

A bit further along the road is "Alick's House", the dairy which supplied milk and eggs around Kirkby and the surrounding areas, to be delivered each morning to the doorsteps by Don, one of the sons of the family. Don was another gentlemen of my childhood; he was always pleasant and extremely respectful. He would allow some credit to build up whereby Mum would pay the weekly bill plus something off the outstanding balance and when he called to the estate on Monday evenings to collect payment and I went to his van to pay him, he always had a smile as he asked after mum. If we ran out of milk it was only a five minute walk to the dairy where we could buy a pint to tide us over until the next day. Don's mother usually answered the door to us and I never felt comfortable calling at the dairy house as I wasn't quite sure if it was the done thing. I didn't realise of course as a child that a business like this, as with the corner shops, wouldn't survive without us, the customers, and our family was quite likely one of the biggest customers of such businesses in Kirkby. The house at the dairy, a very pretty cottage, is still there today, occupied by the daughter of the family.

That takes us to the the end of Kirkby in this direction, the next building up, past the fields, is the Pear Tree Inn which I will mention again later when I relate one of the Kirkby ghost stories as told to me.

Heading back now and across the road from the dairy, past North Park Road to Sefton Drive on the right, at the top of Sefton Close, I can see the first of the private houses built on the edge of our estate in the late 1960s.

I have now walked down Sefton Drive and arrived at

Sefton Close where for mum, dad and Julie aged just two weeks, it all began.

Chapter Three

Settling down

Mum and Dad were married on a cold November afternoon in 1941 in what remained of the Blessed Sacrament Church on Walton Vale in Liverpool, following the "May blitz" of that year. With dad working in the Civil Service as a factory inspector for the Ministry of Food, mum helped her father in the family grocery shop as well as continuing to call at the family home in Firdale Road, Walton, to keep house for him and her two younger brothers and sister. Mum's mother had died two years earlier, following years of ill health due to a heart condition and it would seem to have suited her father to keep things as they were as he asked mum and dad to postpone their wedding. They agreed to this but as time passed by dad eventually put his foot down and insisted that mum be free to marry. My grandfather wasn't too happy at losing his housekeeper and as mum's sister, May, was ten years younger than mum, it would be hard for her to cope. A rift developed between mum and her father but their relationship was patched up in time for the wedding.

A few years after mum and dad were married, Auntie May went to live in America. She actually went to Australia first to stay with relatives but she wasn't happy there so decided to try America. This was arranged by her father, our grandfather, and so she settled in America for several years.

My first memory of Auntie May was when she returned home when I was five, to tell mum of her plans to marry. I can still see her as a young woman with long dark hair, standing with her back to me as she was talking to mum on the landing as I played in the bedroom, wondering why they were arguing and why mum looked sad. It turned out that Auntie May was marrying a widower, a lot older than her. He had grown up children so perhaps it was understandable that mum was a bit disappointed. They did marry and we all became very fond of Uncle Joe when the family returned home to live in the UK after the birth of their first son, Dennis.

Standing: Uncle Eddie, Auntie May, Dad, Mum, Uncle Mick, Grandad.
Seated: Granny, Auntie Maureen

When Julie was born, twelve months after mum and dad were married, she was evacuated with mum to a nursing home in Southport where they stayed for two weeks. Then two days after she returned home to Ince Avenue in Anfield, where they were staying with dad's family, dad was transferred to work at the Royal Ordnance Factory in Kirkby. The rural site in Kirkby had been chosen to minimise any danger of damage to the area surrounding the factory in the event of an explosion. Sadly, there was an explosion over a year later, on 22 February 1944 as one of over 12,000 fuses in the process of being filled at the factory detonated causing the death of one woman and injuring another. I have read that the George Cross was awarded to a Factory Development Officer who, together with three other volunteers, worked solidly for three days to remove the remaining 12,000 fuses from the badly damaged building to safety, to remove the danger of further explosions. I have also heard of the horrendous injuries suffered by other workers at the factory during the course of their work.

Dad's transfer came about following the bombing and closure of The Royal Arsenal at Woolwich, when operations where transferred to the Kirkby factory. Key workers from Woolwich were relocated to Kirkby, where some of them stayed when the war was over.

Two hundred houses were built for the key munitions staff, on what became the Kirkby Park estate where mum and dad were allocated a one bedroomed upstairs flat in Sefton Close. Then when Gerry was born two years later, they moved into a three bedroomed house round the corner in Park Road. The estate was set within a small cluster of privately owned houses, most of which are now listed buildings.

The estate houses were brick built and much the same as any other house of the era apart from having a completely flat roof. The flat roofs were a war effort to save costs and also because the buildings themselves were only ever intended to remain for the duration of the war, as was the ROF factory. Prefabricated wooden huts, known locally as "the hostels", were built on a plot of land at the edge of our estate to serve as homes for a workforce of 1,000 people, the majority of whom were women who travelled into Kirkby from the surrounding areas such as Ormskirk as well as from Liverpool. Gradually, some of these workers began to move to live closer to the factory, marking a change in the population figures in Kirkby which had remained at around 3,000 for the past hundred years or so.

During that first two weeks after Julie was born, dad had taken mum out for a bus ride to Kirkby one Sunday afternoon to show her their new country home where they hoped to leave the destructions of war time just ten miles away in Walton. And so they settled, with dad employed at the munitions factory and mum a wartime housewife who thought nothing of pushing the pram as far as Fazakerley to catch a bus to Walton to visit and to continue helping out her family each week.

The factory subsequently closed down in 1946 having produced ten per cent of Britain's ammunition throughout the war. Whenever I think about that fact, I picture an endless silence.

Kirkby at that time was made up of St Chad's Church with a collection of surrounding farms and houses. The original St Chad's chapel is believed to have been built on the site in the year 870 AD with the existing church having been built a thousand years later. After passing through generations of different families, the Molyneux family became the major landowners in Kirkby during the 16th century, residing at Croxteth Hall. The family were devout catholic and remained so through the Reformation up until their conversion to the Church of England on the marriage of Charles William Molyneux in 1768. Three years later he was given the title of Earl of Sefton. When the seventh and last Earl of Sefton died in 1972, Croxteth Hall was bequeathed to Liverpool Corporation, after a worldwide search failed to find an heir.

That is Kirkby as it was, unchanged in hundreds of years, to be woken up when in 1952 Kirkby "new town" was to develop to re-house some of the overspill of Liverpool, with the population reaching its peak at around 50,000 over the following 20 years. Today the headcount is around 40,000.

Our estate was left untouched and separate from the other Kirkby districts for another twenty years, tucked away behind the railway line. Then, towards the end of the 1960s private developers started to chip away at the boundaries when a road was made through the wasteland at the top of Sefton Close and thirty two new houses were built. That area is now Sefton Drive which had previously been our playing field, used by all the children of the estate and as I am standing here, it isn't too difficult to close my eyes to be transported back.

I can see us playing on the dry, scorched grass from sunny days during the long summer holidays from school, where the grass was kicked away where we played football, cricket and rounders. The field was one of several designated meeting places we had around the estate and at any given time there could be a game in progress, children running to meet friends or to go cycling if a bike ride was the plan.

The field was special as it was here that we all gathered every bonfire night to burn the wood and debris collected during the October half term holidays. We never worried that the fire wouldn't burn, no matter how wet the wood was - we would just throw a bit more paraffin on the already fuel drenched pile. We carried bits of fallen trees, broken wooden boxes and anything that would burn, sopping wet or dry, from all around the estate to make a massive bonfire which could be ten foot high and almost as wide, depending on how much we could collect. We baked potatoes on the fire although I don't ever remember actually managing to eat one that wasn't burnt as black as coal on the outside and hard as rock inside. I can almost taste one now as I rummage through my bag for some mints, but it isn't a bad taste. After the bonfire we would head for home where dad would supervise our own firework display in our back garden. The "bangers" and "rip raps" would have been following us round for weeks, set off by the boys hiding in the entries between the houses or lurking behind a shed on the lookout for a girl to scare.

Another, smaller field on the other side of the road was surrounded by trees and bushes where we picked blackberries to take home for mum to bake in pies. This field is where I ran to once or twice when I left home between the ages of twelve and fourteen after a telling off from mum and dad. I thought I'd teach them a lesson on how to appreciate me by disappearing for a while and wait to see them running round frantically looking for me, full of remorse. The fact was that I soon got bored on my own and never stayed longer than five minutes which was just enough time for me to calm down.

Considering the original purpose of these houses, the estate didn't look too bad, as some effort went into the layout, with each house having fair sized gardens at the front and back. Sefton Close is shaped a bit like an exclamation mark with the houses on either side of the road, leading up to a grass covered island with a footpath through the centre and the houses continuing around it in a circle.

I'm standing now on a road which has replaced that footpath. The planning office could well have got the idea for the road after watching our John if they had seen him riding his moped over the path, saving himself the two seconds it would take to ride round the island. John didn't bother much with rules as he had his own set.

I'm about to walk around the estate now. All the memories, happy, sad or funny as well as pride and every emotion, now woven into the fabric that made me who I am, are here, along with some of the friends and characters I will introduce as I walk round.

I'm standing outside the flat where mum and dad first lived in wartime Kirkby when rationing, "stretching", "improvising" and "make do and mend", were the order of the day. All practices that would stand mum in good stead over the next 20 years as we, the rest of her eight children, made our appearance into the world. Julie told me they kept hens in the garden here during the war as did lots of people but mum was too scared of the hens to collect the eggs and once spent a whole afternoon trapped upstairs by a hen sitting at the bottom of the stairs. Julie, as a tiny tot, wasn't afraid and went into the garden in the mornings to ask the hens to lay her an egg for her breakfast.

I wonder what made up mum's fabric and what gave her her coping strategy. When I listened to stories of her own childhood, which mum seemed to enjoy telling as much as I enjoyed listening to, fascinated by how life was "in the olden days", I pictured a comfortable, quiet family life. She talked of her two brothers and of how the younger one, Jack, had died when I was five. I remember that time when his pregnant wife, Auntie Betty and their two children Ann and Brian came to stay with us for a while. Other stories were of her life in general, the school she went to in Evered Avenue in Walton, where she never professed to be any great scholar, although I think mum didn't give herself credit for just how bright she was. She used to laugh at her academic abilities, saying she only needed to be able to write the shopping lists and add up the cost, but she was capable of very much more than that.

I learned during these chats, the cause of the scar mum had all down the front of her calf when as a twelve year old girl, a kettle boiled over on the stove on the fireplace, the burn being made worse by the black dye from her stocking seeping through. Other stories were of how her mother was a tailoress and mum would sometimes go to bed to be woken the next morning to see her mother had made new dresses or even coats for her.

Auntie Betty & Uncle Jack's wedding
Mum seated (right) with Julie on her knee
Grandad on her left and Auntie May her right

When mum married dad with his very respectable civil service job, she had no reason to believe her lifestyle would change. It did change though during the course of the years it took to have eight babies and although we did see the hardships mum and dad had to bear, I never saw any signs of insecurity in mum and she never seemed to be afraid of anything or anybody. She once told me her own mother was the best friend she had ever had and it may be that the security of her childhood set her up for life. All that didn't stop mum from worrying - she could have won prizes for that.

Dad's childhood, spent partly in Tipperary, was very different from mum's and it was only when I watched the film of "Angela Ashes" that I realised why he never wanted to take us to Ireland. Whenever I asked him he said we wouldn't like Ireland and that it was "In the middle of God's speed". I'm not sure why he used that expression but the film opened my eyes as to why running around the forty shades of green when dad was a boy wasn't all that I had thought.

By the time the country was back on its feet in the 1950s into the 60s when we had "never had it so good", jobs were aplenty and people were able, for the first time in a long time, to aspire to the nicer things of life. The idiom, "Keeping up with the Joneses" came into its own again and our estate was no exception.

Most mothers of young children were housewives who didn't go out to work at that time, meaning for the women of our estate, like others throughout Britain, the most part of their interaction with the outside world was through the neighbours, over the garden fence, or stories brought home by the rest of the family. Mum didn't gossip with the neighbours but whenever we walked in from work her first words would often be, "Any news?"

One of our neighbours, Mr White or "Old Cough Spit", as I heard a neighbour call him, ungraciously, after hearing him out in the back garden in the mornings, would have seen more of the goings on on the estate than most. I believe he kept his own counsel on whatever he heard as I never heard him say a bad word about anyone. He and his wife were retired and always had a friendly smile for us. The road wouldn't be complete without seeing him leaning on his gatepost, smoking the pipe his wife wouldn't allow inside the house. He liked a chat, so it suited him to spend hours outside where passers by were happy to stop. He kept a cockerel which some of the neighbours complained about as it woke them up in the mornings. They should have counted themselves lucky that they didn't live next door to us then they'd have known what noise was.

It was here on the estate that I hit someone for the first time, a girl that I'd never liked who lived in Sefton Close. There's a difference between someone being sad or miserable and she was always so miserable that I don't remember her ever having anything good to say. It was as I was passing by with my friend Pauline who was at the same school as her that they stopped to speak and she made a comment about our family being poor. Without stopping to think, my hand just came up and I slapped her in the mouth as I told her to shut her gob. Her dad came round to complain to mum later but as she had no witnesses apart from Pauline who would be on my side, I denied hitting her and got away with it.

Then round the corner in Park Road is where I hit someone for the second and last time. One of our neighbour's granddaughters used to come to stay during school holidays and I happened to be passing the house as she was arriving for one of her visits. I groaned to myself when I saw her and would have been happy to leave it at that but she stopped me and asked me point blank how many of us there were now in the family. When I asked her why she was asking she said that my mum was greedy because she had so many babies and how every time she visited her gran, we had another baby. So I slapped her in the face and went home feeling quite proud of how I had handled her, while defending the family honour, aged nine. It only took a few minutes for her gran to come over, rat a tat tatting on the front door. Mum, who had been busy scrubbing the kitchen floor with a tin bucket and scrubbing brush when the knock came, stood up and went wearily to answer the door. I kept out of sight but heard muffled voices before mum returned and without uttering a single word, she took me by the arm and pulled me, as I was dragging behind trying to think of how I could redeem myself, across the road where she proceeded to slap the top of my leg in front of the girl and her grandmother. I was mortified. The smacking made my leg sting but that didn't go anywhere near the pain of the sheer humiliation I felt as I stood before the girl and her grandmother.

We had another family of visitors to the estate during the summer holidays each year who we looked forward to seeing for their two week stay as we were the best of friends. They were the Bucks, they came from South Shields and the family was made up of two boys and one girl, Glynis. It was Mrs Buck's widowed father and her brother, Danny that they stayed with, who were living in the end house across the road from us. Hearing their Geordie accent was fascinating and the expressions they used made us laugh - such as being sent to the shop for a "cut lorf" and to get told off was "to get wrong". We never saw much of the granddad who didn't leave the house very often apart from occasionally sitting outside the side door on a warm day. He was taken care of for the most part by Danny until he died during the late 1960s.

As Gerry was coming home at about 1.00 o'clock in the morning after a night out, when Danny was living alone, he saw smoke coming from an upstairs window in the house. He called the fire brigade who found Danny unconscious in an armchair downstairs. He had been smoking in bed after having had a drink and when the bed covers caught fire he had stumbled downstairs. He survived the fire but if it hadn't been for Gerry and if nobody else had seen the smoke, then it could have been a different story.

I hear occasionally of the people I knew from all those years ago who still live here, like Mr Trussell, the father of Monica's best friend from the estate, Christine. Monica met him recently and he's still here after surviving his wife. The parents of my best friend from the estate, Pauline Bolton from next door, who we called to see a couple of years ago have sadly both since died.

As I'm walking to the end of Sefton Close I remember the post box at the top of Park Road and wonder if it's still there. It is - and I feel as if I'm looking at an old photograph as I look at it, having served the estate for more than 60 years. It is actually a replacement box and has been moved a few feet away but people walk the same paths as we did to post their letters. In fact I'm struck by just how much the place feels the same. It's so peaceful here. It's a Friday afternoon and people are coming and going and working in their gardens but the pace seems so slow. This is Kirkby in 2011 but it feels the same as it did 50 years ago. A Shangri la in the middle of Kirkby? - maybe not, but there is definitely some magic here - I always felt it.

The atmosphere might be the same but the roads sound different to how they used to. The sound of people chatting, mingled with the noise of traffic from the main roads has replaced the sounds of the fifties and sixties when it was garden swings we heard, bicycle bells or the sound of metal wheeled roller skates clanking over the pavements. I can't hear children playing today. I can hear their voices as part of the background, amongst the adult voices and the traffic.

Another difference is that the smoking chimneys have gone. There were one or two houses with coal fires still burning away when I last lived here which was always a comforting sight to come home to. The smoke from coal actually disappeared following the Clean Air Act of 1956 when we had to buy coke instead which was more expensive but easier on our lungs and the planet.

On my left now is where Sefton Close meets Park Road, where the Hornes family lived and the place where I did just about the most stupid thing of my childhood. Their front garden was surrounded by a very low brick wall, known to us simply as "Hornes' wall", another of our meeting places. There was one son in the family, Winston, who was a few years older than me so I didn't have much to do with the family but they were always pleasant and never complained about us hanging round their wall.

We were bored and trying to decide what to play one afternoon. I was with Pauline Bolton, Margaret, Monica, Christine Trussell and a couple of their friends. Pauline was lying on the wall with her eyes closed when she asked us if she looked dead. We said we thought she could look more dead so she went on to practice lying as motionless as possible and when we thought she had it just right she asked me to go and tell her mum she was dead - so I did. I knocked on the Bolton's door, looked Mrs Bolton in the eye and said, "I'm sorry Mrs Bolton but Pauline's dead on Hornes' wall." I came back to earth as she pulled the pinny she was wearing up over her face and ran screaming down the road as I ran after her shouting that I was only joking.

We got carried away and were incredibly stupid but we hadn't set out to frighten anybody, unlike Michael, the boy who lived across the road who used to deliberately terrify us. He once spent a whole afternoon running after us with a knife saying he was going to kill us. I was petrified but when I told Julie later she seemed surprised although not unduly bothered and said that Michael was OK, he would have been just pretending. When he grew up and entered the Church of England as a vicar I thought that perhaps Julie may have been right but still had my doubts, as he had a demonic look in his eye that day.

Then there was the Linley family who emigrated to South Africa, holding a street party before they left, inviting all the children from our road except us. Mum said she wouldn't have wanted us to go anyway and was glad to see the back of the snobs and I agreed with her. Mrs Linley once called me from playing in the road when I was about eight, asking me to peel some carrots for her, saying she would give me a present when I had finished. It was a strange request which I didn't want to do but didn't know how to refuse so I sat on her doorstep with a colander and huge bag of carrots for what seemed like hours. I was getting worried the longer I sat there with no sign of Mrs Linley who was indoors, and I was too scared to just go home. She came out eventually and said, "Are you still here? That'll do, you can go now". No present was offered.

The Barnes family lived across the road with their son and daughter, Sam and Shirley. Mrs Barnes, who worked at the Jacobs biscuit factory in Aintree, kept a tin of unwrapped Club biscuits in her kitchen. This was unknown luxury in our house as we never saw a Club biscuit, not even at Christmas. Occasionally Shirley would let us in while her mum was at work and pass the biscuits round. The biscuits were one of the two reasons why I would call on Shirley, who was a couple of years older than me and we didn't have much in common. The other reason was that she could always be relied upon to have a bike in good working order because she hardly used hers.

While it was snowing one winter's day we joined the boys from the estate in putting snow through letterboxes and Mrs Barnes seemed to think we had picked on her and took exception to it. Apparently she had new hall carpet as Mr Barnes informed us when he called later to report our antics to mum. He was a very nice, friendly man and was quite apologetic, telling us his wife was of a nervous disposition. She didn't send him to call on anyone else, just us.

John played with Sam, along with everyone else he came across because everyone was John's "mate". You'd ask him at the end of the day who he'd spent the day with and were always told, "me mate", even if it was someone he'd met that day. He was a genial soul. They had been playing cricket in the Barnes' back garden one afternoon with bricks instead of a ball when, not surprisingly, John was hit on the head. Sam came hurtling down the road screaming that Johnny had split his head open. We were terrified and I never saw mum run so fast but it turned out to be nothing more than a bruise he'd sustained.

Mr and Mrs Wilson lived in the next house along with their two sons. Michael, the younger boy, was a good friend of John's and they still keep in touch. Mrs Wilson used to turn the radio up very high sometimes and if the window was open the tunes of the day would be heard drowning out raised voices amid comments from the neighbours about the

Wilsons being "at it again". I last saw Michael in person when I left home but had a call a few years ago from Monica to tell me to put the television on because he was on "The Weakest Link".

I've come to our house now and am looking up at the two windows in "our room". As little girls Margaret and I would choose a window each to look through in the mornings while lying in bed to see who could count the most birds flying by. Somebody I once told this to said he didn't think they had birds in Kirkby. I wish I had been able to answer him as I would now with a bit more knowledge behind me, that a branch of zoology, namely Ornitology, had listed over one hundred rare and interesting birds in a study carried out at Kirkby, not to mention the Pigeon House, named after a bird in 1703. Perhaps less impressive is the fact that the first pubs of Kirkby new town were named The Falcon, The Fantail, The Golden Eagle, The Kingfisher and The Peacock. Years later those same windows were look out posts for vetting boyfriends. If one of us had someone calling to pick us up then the rest of us would sit on the window sills to get a good view. It was embarrassing sometimes to walk down the path having to explain away the laughter coming from the upstairs windows.

Today there are two young women, one of them holding a baby, sitting on the doorstep in the spring sunshine. The door is open and I can see the kitchen, our kitchen, but without the scrubbed pine table and dresser which have been replaced with glossy white units. This feels so strange, I visit this house so often in one of my recurring dreams where I walk through that same doorway. Nostalgia is starting to merge into regression as I move on.

Our house - 2012

The corner shop was just across the road from our house, in the downstairs corner flat with Mr and Mrs Barton as the proprietors when we were little. I walk past the shop, now restored to a flat, and past where the Barton's lived. They were the only ones on the estate to have a piano and I once overheard Mrs Barton saying that she didn't have enough space to put all her Christmas cards as the piano was full. I don't recall them ever saying they could play the piano. She seemed to think the piano would impress people but it didn't impress me any more than seeing her pop to the shops in Liverpool in her fur coat on Tuesday afternoons on their half day closing.

Mum had a fall out with Mr Barton when she once commented on the price of something in his shop being a bit high and Mr Barton replied, "Your trouble is that you like the best but don't like paying for it". Mum was hurt and never went into the shop herself again but she did send us. Mr and Mrs Barton were always very nice to us and they often asked after mum but she never had an apology. Up until this incident mum would call into the shop every day for her messages, it was so handy and she could leave the older children for a few minutes. That was until the day one of the neighbours went running into the shop to tell mum her curtains were on fire. Gerry and Eddie had been playing with matches and had set fire to the bedroom curtains. Another time they made a bonfire from rolled up newspapers and lit it under mum and dad's bed, on top of the lino.

Mrs Lawson lived at the end of this row. We would catch sight of her looking out of her bay window while we were playing, then once she had seen us she would appear in the doorway to send us on a message to the shop. The busy housewives often did this and paid us a couple of pennies for going. We didn't understand when we were little that Mrs Lawson's protruding eyes were due to a thyroid condition. I wish I had known because although she was so kind to us we were wary of her staring eyes. At other times she would call us over to give us a bag of broken biscuits she had bought from Bartons. Biscuits were weighed out from large, heavy glass jars into half pounds or pounds and when it came to the end of the jar, the biscuits at the bottom were broken and sold off for coppers.

Back to our house now, on the crossroads with South Park Road, leading to the old private houses I've already mentioned, including Waverley House, where I can see Monica has parked on the road outside. I pass on the way the house where Mr and Mrs Robertson lived with their one daughter, Carol. They were certainly always pleasant and friendly but Mr Robertson had a high opinion of himself and we had to make sure we weren't too friendly in return or he could misinterpret it. Eddie tells me the lads used to tie cotton to the Robertson's letter box then run round the corner to pull it, time and again but the Robertsons never saw the cotton when they opened the door to an empty doorstep. Monica says they'd all be given ASBOs if it was today. There was a bit of a commotion outside their house one Saturday afternoon when Mrs Robertson could be seen pacing up and down their garden path, looking agitated and asking everyone around had they seen her husband who was late home from work. When she eventually saw him sauntering down the road after having stopped off at the Railway, she shouted to him to hurry up and put his suit on because, "Our Carol's getting married."

I'm with Monica now and we've walked down to one of the houses a bit further down the road, Ivy Lea, as we've spotted a For Sale board outside. The house can be seen from the footpath a lot more clearly now than when we were children as the ivy which no doubt gave the house its name, has been cut back and the paintwork is in better condition now than it was 40 years ago. The house looks impressive rather than dark and creepy as it did then when I believed one lady lived there with her fifty cats. The adjoining house definitely had a dog roaming loose which would bark when I walked past every morning on my way to school and I would hurry past, not running in case it ran after me, with my heart in my mouth. Then one day I saw it wore a muzzle and my heart stayed put.

Kirkby Tenants Children's Party - late 1950s

Turning back again and walking to the other end of South Park Road, we come to the site of the old Kirkby Tenants Association building on Mount Road. This was a licensed social club in the evenings but by day it served as a mother and baby clinic on Tuesday mornings, where we would collect the free orange juice for children of pre school age for mum during the school holidays. On Tuesday evenings the club was used for the Kirkby Girls' Club, run by

Miss Blake and her assistant, Mrs Thornton. The Club was an opportunity for the girls to meet up and was the only social event available to us. We would regularly join other groups throughout Liverpool to be entered into singing competitions held in St George's Hall. I don't remember us ever winning anything for singing and don't think we ever expected to but it was a day out and quite something to sing on stage at St George's Hall. One of the girls, however, Maeve Wilton, did win a prize in an "English Speaking" contest. She had the most amazing speaking voice which was as clear as a bell and impressed the judges so much that she was voted the winner for the whole of Liverpool.

For the remainder of the time, the premises were used as the social club providing an avenue of entertainment for the adults on the estate as well as an enterprise for the children, who collected the empty pop bottles or played with the beer barrels hanging around outside. We passed the club on our way home from primary school and joined in with the other children who would already be hanging round. The boys would forage through looking for the empty pop bottles to redeem the penny deposit from Barton's shop. I didn't get involved with the wheeling and dealing but did play with, or in, the beer barrels. The club stood on a bit of a hill with enough of an incline for the barrels to be rolled down, with one of us inside, as we took it in turns to climb in and let ourselves be pushed away. I was terrified each and every time I climbed inside a barrel but couldn't let the boys know, as I took my turn each time telling myself I'd have just one more go. The pleasure was in getting out of the barrel in one piece at the bottom of the hill, knowing it was over and not having to listen to the boys shout, "Yer yeller!"

Mount Road was most likely named after that little hill, with Sefton Close being named after the Earl of Sefton from the Molyneux family. The "Park" Roads were perhaps named after the estate itself although there wasn't actually a park around.

A few doors down from the clubhouse, on Mount Road, lived the Masons, a family of three children, two girls and one boy, Michael, with their mum and dad. I never had much to do with the family apart from when a group of us would go for a bike ride and Michael would join in. He was once trying to insist that his bike was better than mine because his had gears even though it was tied together with string. I could see the father of the house through the window most times I passed, sitting in an old vest, looking the worse for wear through drink. I felt sorry for his wife who worked hard at keeping up appearances and was probably accustomed to a better lifestyle than she was having now, which was something she seemed to accept with a degree of bitterness. One day after we'd been on a bike ride, Michael invited us into the house to play while his mum and dad were both out. We only went into each others houses on special occasions such as birthday parties and had never been inside the Mason's house, so we knew it was out of bounds but as both parents were out at the time, we weren't worried. Mrs Mason came home unexpectedly to find half a dozen local children in the house including me and Margaret. She took one look at the two of us and roared at Michael asking what we were doing there and telling him to get us out. Just us two.

I met one of the daughters thirty five years later, through my work. She had bought the family home in Kirkby after both her parents had died and since sold it on and moved to a different, more up market area of Merseyside. She didn't seem to hold any of the prejudice her mother had had and could often be heard in the office referring back to her childhood days and talking about "Daddy".

We turn right now into North Park Road and as with South Park, the private houses are at the top. An apartment block stands on the right hand side, on the site of the bluebell woods of my childhood, although an earlier building had been a convent in the late 1970s which ran a children's day nursery. An air raid shelter once stood in the centre of the woods but I never ventured inside, believing and hoping it to be overrun with ghosts. This was enhanced by an empty, dilapidated old house next to the woods which was later demolished to give way to individual garages rented out to residents of the estate. A notice on the surrounding fence to the house advised of the forthcoming demolition of the building and it was with great excitement that everyone, children included as it was during school holidays, gathered round to watch as the demolition men turned up. We were so disappointed when the house was down so quickly there was nothing really to see, apart from the dust, when we had thought we could make a day of it.

North Park Road 1950

The local GP, Dr Katy, lived opposite the bluebell woods. She had originally worked with her father, Dr Ainsworth and then continued in the practice when he retired. Mum and dad had originally registered with Dr Katy but transferred to Dr Levy in Fazakerley until he retired, as dad apparently wasn't too impressed with Dr Katy. In fact he called her "the vet" which I know doesn't sound respectful and no doubt he had his reasons but whether or not they were justified I'll never know. And so we had to travel the three miles to Fazakerley to see Dr Levy, instead of being able to walk to the top of the road, as indeed Dr Levy had to travel if ever he was called out on a home visit. I asked Julie recently if she knew what had happened between dad and Dr Katy and Julie said that nothing happened, dad just didn't like her. Following Dr Levy's retirement, whenever we visited our new doctor, we would see him through a haze of smoke as he always had a cigarette on the go throughout a consultation.

Having gone full circle we come to a block of flats built in the late 1960s on the site of where the chip shop once stood, serving our estate and the surrounding pre-existing houses and then later, Westvale in the new town. There was also a ladies hairdressers here called Kings, inside a tiny building about the size of our shed.

Site of King's Hairdressers and the chip shop

We turn and look to the left now, across the railway line, overlooking Whitefield Drive in Westvale. This is the land which now houses the replacement Kirkby Station building and is the site where, during the 1960s and early 1970s the mobile shops traded. The mobiles were a Godsend in the days of all shops closing by 5 o'clock, if you happened to have run out of essentials such as bread, tea or cigarettes. They charged exorbitant prices, even higher than the corner shops but as they stayed until 10 o'clock at night it was such a relief to see the mobile as you turned the corner, that we didn't mind paying extra.

A tree lined cinder path, known as the hostel or "ossie" path, separated our estate from the hostels where the ROF factory workers had lived during the war and we're walking along the side of the railway line now, towards the grounds where the hostels have been replaced with an estate of newly built private houses. The memory of this place has always been very special to me and although the innocuous, if dour looking collection of huts may have now disappeared after finally outliving their use after 50 years, I remember them clearly. The ROF site at Kirkby is history, remembered and talked about locally by the people who were around during the war.

After the war, however, the small British town of Kirkby became known in a place much further afield. Eight thousand miles away in fact, in Malaya, when from 1951 until 1962 the Government of the Federation of Malaya (now Malaysia) established a teacher training college on the site and this is where the students stayed for their two year visit. This was the first time any world government had set up its own college in Britain with around 2000 students in total passing through the gates. The whole of the college curriculum was carried out within the grounds, where the students and lecturers also lived, in the black huts which served them well for the duration of their stay.

The students, from differing backgrounds, would most likely all have been expecting something more grand looking than what looked more like a prison camp than their new homes and you have to feel for them when they first saw their bleak surroundings. The pipes were an eyesore but they carried hot water around the site and no doubt the students were grateful for the warmth they provided. In fact the students were very well cared for during their stay.

The college had a deep ditch running part way along the path with more water pipes running through with a bank of trees behind the ditch. One of these trees, an oak tree, was another meeting place for boys and girls alike. At the end of a day we'd run home calling to each other where we were going to meet up the following day, "the old oakie" being one such place. It was a good tree to climb and not too high to get to the broad branches which were sturdy enough for a few of us to sit on at a time.

My memories of the students, contrary to their living accommodation, are of sunshine and smiles as they walked towards the college gates, slowly, chatting amongst themselves. The women were beautiful in their colourful saris in contrast to the drab clothes worn by the local women. Their dark shiny hair would be visible, again so different from the turbaned head scarves the housewives wore indoors, exchanged for dreary looking felt hats for outdoors, pinned to their hair by hat pins.

The entire area which made up the Kirkby Park estate before any redevelopment was something of a mismatch of buildings. Regardless of how well planned our five roads were, the houses were still the odd looking, square, flat roofed boxes, a bit like Lego in fact, set in their pretty gardens with a grass verge, surrounded by a mixture of both modest and grand looking Victorian buildings.

Our houses were identical from the outside apart from the colour of the doors which were painted by the council, as often as every two years, in successive colours of either green, red, blue or yellow. Waverley House, the largest and grandest looking of all the buildings, wouldn't have looked out of place set in Wuthering Heights. Add to the picture the collection of black wooden huts with a network of jet black water pipes running overhead, to complete the blot on the landscape.

Malayan Teacher Training College

I didn't see it like that though when I was a child. To me, anywhere that looked out of place or different was something to be explored and the college grounds were just such a place. It was here that I met and befriended while talking through the college gates, a little Malayan girl called Zaleha, Leha for short. Her father was a lecturer at the college when we were both aged six to seven and I felt privileged to be allowed inside the gates to play. I never saw any of the other local children in the grounds, which may well have been because they weren't interested as there wasn't much to do in the grounds and there were not many children. Leha wasn't allowed to play outside the college so we amused ourselves by generally playing around, swinging on the water pipes, or looking for ghosts. There was a brick built air raid shelter inside the grounds, close to the entrance which, like all the remaining shelters I came across, I was sure must be teeming with ghosts. We spent one afternoon staring through the window of an empty building at the college on the lookout for a ghost when we both claimed to have seen a round light the size of a tennis ball floating round. There was definitely something I saw but am not sure if it was a trick of the light and I didn't know if Leha was making it up but this was long before the days we had ever heard about orbs.

I was invited regularly into Leha's home to meet her parents and to talk to them. Being asked my opinion by adults who appeared to listen to what I had to say was a rare experience at the age of six, as I sat there being passed cups of tea. Outside the college gates, or outside our house, if we were spoken to by some of the not very friendly neighbours it was usually to tell us to clear off.

It was these talks with Leha's family that gave meaning to the geography lessons I was to have a couple of years later, when I could conjure up pictures of the characters I read about in foreign lands, having already had an introduction. When I was eight I was given a book to read in school, called, "Bombo's Land" which I think was actually set in South America. The book described Bombo's life of short school days in the hot weather, playing on the beaches, catching fish for tea and playing in his tree house. I imagined Malaya to be like that and thought of it as paradise.

My friendship with Leha ended suddenly when the family returned to Malaya as I was only told they were going home a few days before they left and we didn't exchange addresses. I was disappointed and missed them for a while and the whole experience was something I was never to forget.

While writing this story I discovered that one of the former students from the Malayan college is now a writer of both academic books as well as fiction, and that he had written a novel based on his time in Kirkby. I couldn't get hold of a copy of the book through sites advertising it on the internet in Malaysia and New Zealand but I did find the author's details so contacted him directly and he sent me a copy. As I looked further I found websites referring to the Kirkby Alumni Association for students from the college, almost 50 years after it closed. I read stories of the fond memories of Kirkby still held by many of those students and also of the Annual General Meeting of the Association in 2009 held in Kuala Lumpur, attended by the Deputy Prime Minister and Minister of Education. The agenda for the AGM of the Alumini Society lists the ex students of the college, referred to as "Kirkbyites", who have attended these gatherings.

The AGM in 2009 saw the launching of the book I now have entitled, *Kirkby: The Life and Loves*, by Dr

Shaari Isa. Shaari was a student at the college from 1953-1955. After leaving the college he returned to Malaya before travelling whilst pursuing his teaching career as well as qualifying as an accountant and gaining a doctorate in that subject. Throughout his career he has always retained a love of writing.

I had originally told Shaari that I had lived close to the college and that I was interested in reading his book, then in a later message I told him how I used to play with a little girl called Leha. I told him this as my way of letting him know that I had had an involvement with the college and that it had meant something to me. I was delighted and amazed when two days later I received a message from him saying he had found a record of Leha and her family from the records of the teaching staff at the college. He had details of her marriage and education and knew that she had spent some time living in Egypt. He said he would get back to me when he had an update so I left him looking for Leha but not expecting any result. A few days later he sent me her email address with an invitation to contact her.

We keep in touch now. Leha has fond but faded memories of Kirkby. She can remember playing in the college grounds and the ghost hunting and says this coincided with a scary television programme showing at the time, the combination giving her nightmares which she took back to Malaya. Her most vivid memory of her time in Kirkby is of the two of us planting flower seeds in their bit of garden outside their house.

I recognised one or two names in Shaari's book. One of them being a neighbour of ours who worked at the college. I told Shaari that I remembered the lady and her family and he has asked me if I could try to contact them as he would like to send a copy of his book to the lady's relatives, who he says, was like a mother to the students when they were so far from home. I have made enquiries to trace the relatives and would hope to be able to pass the information on to Shaari before long.

I have a couple of stories surrounding the college as told to me by my brothers recently. The first one, from Gerry, is something I'm quite glad I didn't know about at the time.

He would be about fifteen at the time when he was riding round on his bike outside the college gates with a couple of friends one Sunday evening. They noticed that the gates weren't locked which was unusual in itself. They went inside to see, leading from the caretaker's building just inside the grounds, down to a recreation hall a couple yards away, a row of coins lying on the ground side by side, forming a line. The boys thought it was some sort of game being played but didn't stay long enough to find out. They did return at the same time on Sunday for the following few weeks to find the gates firmly locked.

The other story comes from Eddie and tells a tale following the closure of the college by the Malayan government, which had been succeeded by a female British teacher training college. He was sitting with Gerry and friends, on the "old oakie", watching the comings and going at the college, which I can imagine to be a regular pastime for the boys as the college was now totally female territory. The Sisters from the convent on North Park Road used to visit the college regularly to take lectures and two of them who happened to be passing, stopped to chat, just as one of the boys was swinging from a branch. Eddie swears it was an accident which caused the string holding the boy's trousers up to snap and his trousers to fall down, to reveal that he wasn't wearing underpants.

Whatever else we lacked by way of clothes, we did have underwear. As our Eddie says, not much went in the bin in those days and mum made use of everything. Once clothes had outlived their purpose they were often recycled into knickers for the girls. You could buy knicker elastic for just such a purpose but the boys in our house, whatever else they were short of, at least had the respectability of shop bought underpants.

"Yes Sir, I'm from Kirkby"

"The Malayan Teachers' Training College in Kirkby, Liverpool, existed for a short eleven years, between 1951 - 1962, but changed the lives of the trainees and the nation, forever."

oooooooooooooooo

150 trainees were selected from thousands each year to attend Kirkby, a college set up specifically to meet the demand for trained teachers in Malaya.

When they first arrived in Kirkby, the students expected it to be a grand building but they were disappointed when they saw the "barracks" with the black heating pipes running all over the place. They quickly cheered up, however, when they saw that the college had central heating. They were worried about the reception they would receive from their hosts, given their colonial history but they found them to be friendly and hospitable and they quickly adapted to their new surroundings which became known as "Kampung Kirkby".

The students had no inkling they were about to become part of history.........

One chilly winters' day on February 7 1956, about 300 students of the Malayan Teacher Training College, Kirkby, Liverpool, were told to assemble in the hall to receive Malayan dignitaries from London.

Moments later, black Humber Super Snipe limousines, decorated with flags drew up at the hall. The then chief minister of Malaya, Tunku Abdul Rahman and the then education minister, Datuk Abdul Razak, alighted from them.

The visit followed meetings of the dignitaries with the British Government. Tunku said that talks had taken place and then made the announcement that we would be getting our independence and that the date would be 31 August 1957. There was a roar in the hall as everybody clapped and cheered.

This was perhaps the first time that that the cries of "Merdaka"/Freedom had been heard on British soil.

ooooooooooooooooo

The returning graduates to Malaya played a part in the early education system of Malaysia and as dedicated teachers, they touched many lives.

In 2001, in her message in a souvenir publication, "The Golden Panduan", Tuanku Bainan had written,

"Kirkbyites can be proud that they played a significant part in the development of teacher education in Malaysia. They have contributed and are still contributing to the progress of the nation and I feel that in recognition of this historic and significant role, some form of permanent record should be thought of to perpetuate the memory of the college......."

On 28 April 2001, Raja Permaisuri Perak Tuaku Bainan Mohdi Ali, signed a declaration on a plaque, naming a college hall at Maktab Pergaran Tuanku Balnun in Penang, Duan - Kirkby.

Extracts of the memories of the "Kirkbyites" were retold in the following article:

KAMPUNG KIRKBY FIRST TO HEAR OF MERDEKA DATE

by Julian Matthews - The Star - 2005

"Another Kirkbyite, ...says, that his best memory of Kirkby was that there was a complete lack of consciousness of class. No-one was Indian, Malay, Chinese, Sikh or Eurasion. We were all Malayans and this is etched in our collective memories. The friendship that we had was something unique. I do not remember any institution where you had this kind of feeling among students. Having come from different backgrounds, we became such good friends and were brothers and sisters there. ..... I can remember going to a local college afterwards and expecting the same warmth but it wasn't there.

If the kind of spirit we kindled in Kirkby could prevail on a larger scale, unity and interaction among nations would be much better today."

Chapter Four

The Estate

As Kirkby's population grew, so did its reputation and mum and dad came to hate the little town where they had settled but they were never able to leave. The "Liverpool Echo" carried regular stories of crime and the mud began to stick. Having their names added to the council "housing list" for a transfer to another area for years, amounted to nothing and buying a house was out of the question.

Kirkby, like other such overspill towns was a disaster in the making. The rapid population growth brought about such problems as a lack of leisure facilities, leaving the youngsters with nothing to do, often unemployed, with no prospects in sight.

By the time I was born, mum, dad, Julie, Gerry and Eddie were established in Park Road and dad had returned to work for the Ministry of Food when the war ended. As mum explained it to me when I was old enough to understand, not only did they have a growing family to feed and clothe but as they had married and set up home eight years earlier, the household goods and furniture needed replacing and it was just too much of a struggle on dad's salary. He needed to earn more and so he made the decision to resign from the Civil Service in exchange for a job as a crane driver on the Liverpool docks.

All the hours God sent were available to work at the

thriving dockland at that time and dad often did indeed work seven days a week. At the end of his first day at the docks he met one of the neighbours, a former colleague, on the train home, who passed a disparaging comment on dad's dirty boiler suit. Dad replied that the money wasn't dirty. He never told me how the comment had actually made him feel but it was a tale he often repeated and whenever we saw a government minister on the television carrying the official ER briefcase, he would remind us as he sat in his boiler suit of how he used to carry such a briefcase. Dad wasn't a government minister and didn't carry a red box but he did carry a brown one inscribed with the royal cypher, "ER" which he was very proud of. Julie keeps a letter addressed to dad which had enclosed two copies of the Official Secrets Act for his signature. I'm sorry dad found himself in the position of having to give up his career in the Civil Service but I could not be more proud of him for taking that decision.

The tenancies of the houses were eventually taken over by the newly formed Kirkby Urban District Council in 1958. Prior to the upgrading project embarked upon by the council, when we moved from next door, the painting of the doors was the only regular maintenance ever carried out. The upgrade didn't improve the outward appearance but such things as general repairs to windows, doors etc. were made and pieces of wood were secured to the stone treads on the staircase. Forty years later the houses were completed by the addition of peaked roofs and the houses, still standing, now 70 years later, look better than ever, the majority of them being privately owned and well maintained.

Shortly after our estate changed ownership and became the property of the newly formed Council, the residents were given a vote with the option of either remaining in Kirkby or transferring to Melling. Mum and dad were delighted at the prospect of living in Melling, a pretty little village with a well respected name. They were very disappointed, however, and could never understand why the majority of the votes went to Kirkby. There was no denying the bad press Kirkby was receiving and I can't imagine who would choose to be associated with the name. If the name had changed, however, our status would also have changed, overnight, and we would have grown up in Melling, the same people with the same lives but with a different name tag. And so it was in Kirkby that we spent our childhood, sheltered to some extent on our small estate, where, away from the more densely populated new areas of Westvale, Northwood and Southdene, life could, at times, be serene.

An Agreement made the ___ day of May 1944.

Between THE MINISTER OF SUPPLY (hereinafter called "the Minister") on behalf of His Majesty of the one part and Edward _____ of 19ᵗʰ Sefton Close, Kirkby in the County of Lancashire (hereinafter called "the Tenant")

of the other part.

Whereby it is agreed as follows:—

1. THE Minister lets and the Tenant takes the messuage or dwelling-house and premises known as 17 Park Rd, Kirkby. in the County of Lancashire (hereinafter called "the said premises") from Monday the Fifteenth day of May 1944 on a tenancy from week to week until determined in accordance with

   the provisions hereinafter contained at the inclusive rent of £ ___ a week the said rent to be payable in advance on Monday in each week the first of such payments having been made on the signature of this agreement: Provided that if the general rates payable in respect of the said premises should be increased or decreased the amount of the inclusive rent payable hereunder shall be increased or decreased accordingly.

2. THE Tenant agrees with the Minister as follows:—

   (a) to pay the said rent on the days and in manner aforesaid clear of all deductions

   (b) to keep the said premises and the fixtures and fittings therein together with the water heating and lighting apparatus and the closet drains and cesspools thereof well cleaned and the chimneys swept as occasion may require and immediately to replace any cracked or broken glass in the windows thereof

   (c) to cultivate the garden forming part of the said premises in a proper and husbandlike manner and to maintain in good condition any fences thereof whether the same be live or dead fences

   (d) not to use the said premises or any part thereof for any purpose other than that of a private dwelling-house

4376. 5 /600

101

As we settled into our new home on the end of the row, the Boltons moved back into their own house, now two doors away from ours, as order was restored. A family new to the estate, made up of four generations of grandmother, son, his son and daughter and her children, moved into our old house next door. The young mother had the responsibility for keeping house and she did seem to work very hard at keeping everything going without much help from the rest of the family. We didn't see a lot of them apart from their coming and going from the house as they appeared to keep themselves to themselves. We heard a lot of them though, through the walls. They hadn't been in the house for long when one evening, while I was lying on my bed reading, I heard shouting such as I'd never heard before from behind closed doors. It was quite frightening with a lot of banging going on but as it became a regular occurrence, it was something we had to get used to whether we liked it or not. If it had been that sort of noise which Mrs O'Mara had had to listen to, rather than the sound of children playing, then she would have been begging us to come back.

It was around this time that we had to take to always making sure the outside doors were firmly closed. Not that we had been given any reason to distrust our new neighbours but whenever the grandmother of the family left the house she had difficulty remembering where she lived. I walked into our hall one day to find Monica staring transfixed at the front door, saying she could see a pair of eyes looking through the letterbox. I thought she was joking at first but when I saw the eyes for myself we were both scared and ran into the front room to tell everyone else. Further investigation by Gerry who opened the front door, revealed the old lady, who we christened "Mrs Red Lid", as we didn't know her name at the time and she always wore a red hat, asking was this her house. We sent her next door but as the episode was repeated almost daily, we made sure the doors were closed. It wasn't just our house she called at, we would often see her wandering up the footpaths to various front doors in her red hat.

As a family we benefited from the Council's

renovation exercise by moving into a bigger house. Quite apart from this, the works also provided the boys on the estate with a source of amusement, such as the arsenal of weapons the workmen left behind at the end of each working day because as we all know, it wasn't necessary to lock doors in those days and open doors were an invitation for the boys to investigate. When Gerry found a Hilti nail gun lying around, he borrowed it to see the effects of firing caps instead of nails, from the bedroom window. It was unfortunate that Mrs Lloyd, whose garden backed onto ours, had just put her washing out to dry at the time, only to see it being potentially destroyed as she watched the cartridges raining down from the window. Dad pacified her when she called round later and as it happened the washing was undamaged, just needing another wash. What was even more unfortunate for all concerned happened just the following day when the boys went into our old garden next door to collect apples from the trees which we still believed to belong to us. Instead of carrying the apples round, the boys threw them over the garden hedge and one of the raining apples accidentally went through Mrs Lloyd's kitchen window.

Gerry was glad to return the nail gun to the workmen's store, as he had always intended to as it was only a borrow. We did hear of at least one of the neighbours who "borrowed" material while the works were ongoing, without any intention of returning it. This family built a brand new garden shed, courtesy of Kirkby Council, from "discarded rubble" collected at the end of the day after the workmen had gone home.

As the last generation of children able to roam free, our home time, school holidays and weekends were spent out playing every waking hour we could. I would go calling with my sisters, starting next door at Pauline's house then round the estate, knocking on doors to see who was playing out. The boys would of course make their own plans which only ever included us in such things as bike rides or when we joined in the occasional game of rounders or cricket. I had school friends down in Station Road in Melling, just a few minutes walk away, but I kept my two sets of friends distinctly separate as school was completely separate from home. I don't remember my best friend from primary school, Tricia, ever even meeting Pauline. Arrangements to meet up later in the day at one of our pre-arranged meeting places would be made if anyone wasn't ready to come out. We were always under strict orders to return home for dinner and would be in trouble with mum if we disobeyed orders.

I ran home reluctantly one day for my lunch to see mum standing on a chair to put the clean net curtains up. She said she would make poached egg on toast for me in a few minutes time. Being in such a rush to get out again I said I could do it myself then went running round the kitchen in such a hurry that I dropped the egg on the floor. I stood looking at it, fuming, and decided to throw the egg in the bin and run out. As I called goodbye to mum she called back something about how quick I'd been, asking if I had eaten my egg. I said I had. Lying to mum played on my mind for the afternoon and when I walked in for tea later I told her what had happened. She said she knew anyway, because she'd seen the egg in the bin. I couldn't lie to mum and besides, honesty was always the best policy because she seemed to know everything.

That's the only time I can remember missing a meal apart from if I was ill. Our diet was made up of healthy and wholesome, good old fashioned English food. The only spices which ever entered our house when we were children would be whatever went into Christmas cakes, Christmas puddings or rice pudding. Mum was an excellent cook and she and dad were very fussy about what we ate. The sausages mum bought had to be the best and not the ones dad said were made up mostly of bread. In the days before food labelling he drew his own conclusions about what went into prepared foods on the shelves. Tinned chicken soup, for instance, was so named according to dad after a chicken was once seen flying over the factory roof.

Remaining skinny despite being amongst the best fed children around, gave the boys something to skit us about, like regularly telling us they'd seen more meat on a butcher's pencil on a Monday morning than on us. Dad could be just as bad and it was something he said which caused me to swear out loud for the first time in my life. I was about twelve at the time and was in the bedroom when I heard dad asking Margaret to go and tell me he wanted to speak to me but what he actually said was, "Where's Skinny Banana Legs, can you go and get her". He'd called me the name before and I had chosen to ignore it but I couldn't this time when I saw Margaret laugh as she repeated it, so I replied, "Well tell him to come and bloody tell me himself." I was scared then and went to shut the bedroom door to hide behind but stopped in my tracks when I heard dad howl with laughter. I closed the door, leaned on it and shouted out every swear word I had ever heard him say.

We once watched a documentary at tea time one evening, showing a tribe of African women who had their necks stretched by putting rings round them while they were still growing. I was always conscious of having a long neck which dad called "swan like" but I just thought of as too long. We were going out to play after tea and I just knew that if the boys on the estate had watched the same programme then they would say something. Sure enough they had watched the programme and started as soon as I went back out, apparently thinking they were hilarious by asking me where I kept my neck rings.

Deciding what to play or do outside involved using our imagination when resources were limited and we needed to beat the boredom. Apart from the organised games of football, cricket or rounders we played the usual outdoor games of skipping, hopscotch, roller skating, riding scooters, playing with hoola hoops, juggling balls, hollies (more commonly known as marbles) and whip and top etc. Then when we wanted something more challenging to do there were some good trees around to climb, or walls to jump off. The most potentially dangerous game I ever played was to see who could jump off the highest wall. We knew all the walls on the estate and surrounding area and progressed to higher ones the older we got, but I jumped off my last wall the time I broke my ankle. Pauline and I were standing on a wall of about ten feet high, just along the road by the college gates. We were holding hands and were to jump on the count of three but we were out of sync with our counting as Pauline went first, pulling me behind her. Luckily for me, Gerry was passing by on his bike and carried me home on the crossbar. Poor mum had to drop everything to take me to Walton hospital along the well trodden path she said she had worn over the years.

A favourite jumping wall

Pauline's garden next door wasn't exactly on the lines of a secret garden but I thought it was pretty special. I've seen photographs taken recently showing the layout has hardly changed through the years with a paved pathway outside the back door and flower beds to each side - and they had rose bushes. They had a sandpit on the paving where we loved to dig tunnels. Much as I loved the flowers, the best part of the garden was a wooden shed that Mr Bolton had built which we were allowed to play in on rainy days. An old chest of drawers had been painted white, along with a couple of old chairs and by the time we had added jam jars full of bluebells and other wild flowers, it was a home from home. We kept busy in our little shed house waiting for the rain to stop by playing board games, reading or other such indoor pastimes as attempting to make perfume from the roses. After cramming the most beautifully scented petals into empty jars before adding water, we waited for it to change to perfume, only to be bitterly disappointed and puzzled each time we tried, as to how we ended up with stagnant water. It's as well that we didn't have the internet then because we would have found out that part of the process actually involves boiling the water and it could well have ended in disaster.

We didn't have the likes of Pauline's shed in our garden but we did have a perfectly good coal shed, which remained empty of coal throughout the summer months. As Pauline and I stood looking into it one such summer's day, we had an idea. The brick built, windowless shed was dark and dirty with coal dust but undaunted, we decided that after a sweep out it would make good storage space. We then had to think of something to store so after some seconds spent brainstorming we came up with the idea of holding a jumble sale with the proceeds to go to charity.

The idea was commendable but unfortunately, in our usual style, we didn't think it through beyond knocking on doors to collect jumble from the neighbours. I felt out of my depth from the start, not really having a clue what we were doing and wanting to tell mum but not knowing how to broach the subject. The more time that went by when I would try to discuss plans for an actual sale with Pauline, she would just shrug her shoulders, telling me not to worry, we would sort it out. Neither of us had ever even been to a jumble sale but we had been to the annual "bring and buy" sale held at the Waverley House summer fayre where they sold good things like cakes and books and I expected a jumble sale to be conducted in much the same way. Being honest with myself I knew there was a difference in what we were selling, which amounted to all the neighbours' junk which if they didn't want then nobody else was likely to. Collecting from the neighbours didn't present any problems as the housewives were only too happy to help the two little girls with the kind hearts. The shed filled up as the weeks went by and as the summer holidays were shortly to come to an end, we still didn't have any plans for a sale.

Eventually I became so worried that I thought I'd

better tell mum what we'd been doing. I'm surprised she or dad hadn't noticed but then they'd had no reason to go into the shed. Mum listened to me and took it seriously but very well. She told me we would have to let the neighbours know that the jumble sale was cancelled and ask them would it be ok to dispose of the goods in the best way we could if they didn't want them back.

I managed to get Pauline to accompany me to one or two houses where we stood babbling something about them wanting their jumble back. We didn't get the same reaction as when we had first called, just a few strange looks as the doors were closed. Pauline's parents remained oblivious while Mum thanked me for being honest, saying that whatever other faults I had, she knew that I always told the truth. I wasn't sure what she meant by my faults but left it at that.

The following summer Pauline and I looked into our empty shed again, with experience on our side, and came up with a better, legitimate idea this time. Along with my sisters and their friends, we decided to turn the shed into a shop - a pretend one. We spent weeks collecting empty food packets, bottles and jars from our mums which were used to line the walls of the shed which looked very impressive as our collection grew. We would then play shop with even the boys joining in, trying to catch us out by asking for something obscure that we didn't have. Whenever we were at a loose end we would get a gang round to pass an afternoon in the shop.

True to form, again, we hadn't planned this through to the end in that we hadn't thought what we would do when the coal men came at the end of the holidays. Then one day while I was in the shed, stocking up the shelves with Margaret and Pauline, we heard what sounded like Monica, Sheila and friends running towards us, screaming something about coal. They arrived breathless in the garden while we stared at them as they managed to get the words out that the coal men were humping sacks onto their backs and would be here at any minute. It was all hands on deck then as we frantically tried to rescue our stock to throw on the grass outside but we were fighting a losing battle as everything was flattened by the men who weren't going to hang around waiting for us, as they dumped the coal, with coal dust flying everywhere. We were a bit disappointed that we had lost our shop but only had to look at each other covered in soot to see the funny side. The shop in the shed had served its purpose and it was time to move on.

A highlight of our summer holidays was the annual visit to the estate of the grass cutting man. Once he was sighted on the estate, word would soon get round and before long the man with his wagon and trailer would look like the Pied Piper of Hamelin. He would go round the estate, cutting the grass verges which surrounded the houses and as the wagon began to fill up with grass, he would let us all climb in. That may sound like a simple pleasure but it's very hard to describe the exhilaration we felt at being bounced around on the back of that cart, in the freshly mown grass, as there's nothing to compare with the sheer joy of it all on an afternoon guaranteed to be fun. They were such simple but happy days.

A regular pastime for the girls from the age of about twelve was to take babies for walks. We would knock on the door of any mum with a baby to ask could we mind the baby and we were never refused. We were never once asked by a mother to take her baby, they always waited for us to volunteer and I can still see the tension in a mother's face begin to fade, knowing she could have a break to get her jobs done. It was a look I'd seen many times on mum's face. The babies never seemed to cry for us as they slept for the most part or gurgled away, being pushed around in the pram.

The regular visits of the rag and bone man were announced by his dulcet tones heralding his arrival, clearing the roads of children playing, as they ran to collect the old clothes and junk at the prospect of a balloon in exchange. Anything with a higher value than the items for scrap would sometimes be exchanged for such treasures as a tea cup. I was always disappointed never to have been given a cup but now realise it was just as well, as mum's pride would never have run to taking cups from the rag man.

While walking along with his cart one very hot, sunny afternoon, the rag man passed Eddie, on his way home from school, carrying a brand new blazer. I don't know the full story apart from that I saw Eddie walk in with a balloon in place of his blazer.

Whether or not he'd had a touch of heat stroke I have no idea but it was totally out of character for him to do anything as daft as that as he was probably the most astute of all of us. Mum ran after the rag man and managed to catch him to retrieve the blazer. I would love to know what she said to him. When I reminded Eddie recently of this story, he said he vaguely remembers but is sure it was a goldfish and not a balloon he exchanged the blazer for. He could well be right there but goldfish -v- balloon - I wouldn't say there's a lot between them compared to a new blazer so don't believe Eddie got such a good deal. Anyway, he asked me not to tell anybody so don't worry Eddie, I won't breathe a word.

I discovered very recently that Eddie still walks along with his eyes to the ground when he had a fascinating find while we were out revisiting old haunts. I'll give more details later.

There was no denying how welcome Kirkby shopping centre was for everybody when it first opened in 1958 as it was no longer necessary to go into Liverpool town to shop now that we had practically everything on the doorstep. With shoe shops, department stores (such as Littlewoods), butchers, bakers, television and electrical goods shops, all our needs were catered for. Supermarkets such as Fine Fare followed where mum began to shop, gradually phasing out the services of the Co-op which had previously supplied the bulk of our groceries. Mum would send us to Fine Fare with a shopping list and a five pound note, asking us to put a piece of elastic on it.

Shopping in Fine Fare, with the advent of supermarkets, was to save me and my sisters from the mortification we had previously suffered on the monthly visits we made to the top shop, to buy the one item we were almost too embarrassed to ask for, especially if there was a man behind the counter. This happened to me more than once when I nearly passed out with embarrassment before leaving the shop empty handed. On one of these visits I walked into the shop to see Pauline hovering at the counter, apparently waiting to be served. I don't know how long she had been there but she was nowhere in sight as I walked up the road on my way to the shop and when I asked her what she was buying, it was obvious from the look on her face that we had both come for the same thing. On these occasions I tried not to speak but would instead look at the assistant with a pained expression, hoping she would read my mind. It worked sometimes as I would with enormous relief see the penny drop, and a look of conspiracy appear, as I was handed the goods wrapped up in last night's "Echo", the wrapping ritual taking far too long. If I did have to speak, it would be in a whisper, with a face as red as a beetroot, as I asked for a packet of "STs".

Mum and dad liked the shops in Walton Vale and continued to visit those shops as well as Freemans clothing shop on County Road. Freemans, along with T J Hughes in London Road in town was one of the participating shops of the "The Provident" credit scheme. Payments were collected and new

115

transactions arranged weekly by a man mum called "the club man" who called at the house. I once overheard a couple of the girls at work talking about asking their mums to "get a cheque" to buy something with and guessed they were talking about the Provident. When I asked, one of the girls looked at me before saying, "It's OK you won't know what we mean". It suited me not to give too much away about myself and I was quite happy letting people think I didn't know anything about the "club man."

Whenever mum travelled by bus to County Road, if she had something awkward to bring home, such as mop buckets or broom handles from the very handy hardware shop she loved to browse through, Monica reckons she always drew the short straw by being asked to accompany mum. They would be sure to bump into one of her friends on the way home and all traces of 1960s "street cred" would vanish when they saw the mop bucket. In fact mum used to describe herself as "Country bumpkin goes to town" whenever she went to town as she said she always did something daft.

Monica's most embarrassing shopping trip was the day mum found an offer on pillows somewhere along County Road, so bought about ten to take home on the bus accompanied by Monica and Margaret. All went well until mum put her pillows down to sort out the bus fare and they blew away only to get stuck under the wheels of a bus which disappeared down County Road with the pillows going round and round the wheels.

I remember that mum would always treat herself to a quarter of nice sweets, such as bonbons or eclairs whenever she went to town and share them with us when she came home.

Kirkby market opened in 1960, which over time was to become the largest outdoor market in the country, selling everything including records, clothes and even second hand shoes, with the largest stall being held by Bob Isherwood, who sold just about everything. The market is still going strong today.

Kirkby's first youth club, Centre 63, was opened in 1963. New pubs and social clubs appeared throughout Kirkby but there was still a lack of recreational facilities for Kirkby's youth throughout the teenage years of a whole generation. The nearest swimming baths were two buses away in Norris Green; six miles away, Maghull had a small cinema to serve its own residents, so Kirkby didn't have a lot to offer, over and above the necessities, for a population of tens of thousands.

MINISTRY OF FOOD
Telephone : ....

Your Ref. ....

M.O.F. Ref. ..NR1/BD.......

NATIONAL REGISTRATION
CITY OF LIVERPOOL FOOD
OFFICE,   N.W. 2B, NHA
WALKER ART GALLERY,
WILLIAM BROWN STREET,
LIVERPOOL. 3.

15th July, 1949.

Dear

Official Secrets Act

With reference to the Official
Secrets Act, I should be glad if you
would sign the enclosed two copies
of the Declaration, one copy to be
kept by yourself, and the other to
be returned to this office, together
with an acknowledgment of the receipt
of your copy.

Yours faithfully,

E. V. M. Vine & a H.

E.V.M. Vine,
Food Executive Officer.

17, Park Road,
Kirkby, Liverpool.

MINISTRY OF FOOD

Recruitment to Established Posts in the Civil Service (Clerical Grade)

ORDER OF ADMISSION

NW

Candidates Reference No. 2-75

This Order will admit you to the written examination on 14th June, 1949 at the centre described below. It must be produced at the beginnings of both mornings and afternoon sessions and at any other time during the examination on request.

You should read the advice below and the regulations overleaf very carefully.

Please write your reference number in the space provided above before you set out for the examination and bring with you writing materials and an addressed economy label (not franked) for notifying the result of the examination. Your reference number should be put boldly at the top of the label.

Address of Examination Centre

4th Floor, Derby House,
Exchange Buildings,   (Chapel St., entrance)
Liverpool 2

Advice to Candidates

i.   The examination will consist of four separate papers and the time table will be

Assembly etc. 10 a.m.
Morning Session English I   10.15 a.m. - 11.35 a.m.
                  Arithmetic 11.50 a.m. - 12.50 p.m.

Afternoon Session English II 2.30 p.m. - 3.50 p.m.
                  General   4 p.m. -   5 p.m.

(Candidates who prefer not to rely upon local facilities for a midday meal should consider bringing a packed lunch)

119

Regulations to be observed by candidates

1. Candidates should lay aside hats, umbrellas, books, etc. or accessories such as slide rules or mathematical tables before taking their seats in the examination room. If possible, a separate room will be provided for this purpose and reasonable precautions taken to safeguard candidates' property but no liability for loss or damage can be accepted by the Ministry. Candidates are advised not to bring with them valuables which cannot be kept on their person.

2. Candidates must bring their own pen and ink and a few ordinary pins. No other accessory will be needed. Fountain pens may be used. Ordinary rulers may be used but slide rules and mathematical tables are prohibited and the supervisor has discretion to prohibit the use of any other accessory.

3. Candidates should attend punctually and preferably ten minutes before each session is due to begin. A candidate who arrives 30 minutes or more after a paper has begun will be refused admission but may return for the next paper. Extra time will not be allowed to late arrivals in any circumstances.

4. Candidates must not leave the examination room without permission, and permission will not be granted (except for such cause as illness) during the first half hour or the last five minutes of any paper. A candidate who seeks permission to leave temporarily, e.g. for illness, should at the same time ask for permission to return and complete the paper. Unless permission to return is given before the candidate leaves the room, re-admission will be refused.

5. Silence must be maintained in the examination room and any candidate who behaves in a disorderly or improper manner may be excluded from the examination.

6. A candidate who attempts during the examination to secure irregular assistance from books, or the papers of other candidates, or any other source, will be disqualified. Similarly a candidate who attempts to give irregular assistance to another will be disqualified.

7. Candidates must write their reference number (not their name) on each answer sheet or piece of paper used, and all papers issued to candidates must be pinned together and handed in – whether it is used or not – before the candidate leaves the room. Portions of papers may not be removed nor any papers be mutilated in any other way.

120

Chapter Five

St Mary's RC Primary School

Mrs Gibbons' infants class - ages five to seven. I am six.

When I first started here there weren't enough desks to go round, so some of us had to make do with a cloth bag to keep our books and pencils in. I had a bag and hated it because every day when I was told to take something out, I had to feel for it while Mrs Gibbons stood over me, telling me to stop rummaging. My rubber and pencil were always getting stuck in the corner and we weren't allowed to leave anything out that we weren't using.

I have an orange box now, covered with a piece of wood for me to lean on, which is so much better. The box is purple but I've seen oranges being taken to the shops in boxes like this so that must be why they call it an orange box rather than a purple one. It's made of thin, splintery wood that scratches me if I'm not careful but I don't mind that because at least

I can take my things out quickly as all I have to do is lift the piece of wood up and I can see everything without worrying about being hit. I've told mum and dad that Mrs Gibbons shouts and mum calls her impatient. I haven't said much about how hard she hits people because I don't want her to know I've told anybody.

I sit on the back row next to Brian Riley. He is eleven.

I don't know why he is still in this class but he has been sitting in that corner ever since I started school. The back row is meant to be for when you are ready to go up to the juniors and he'll be leaving the school this year to go to St Bede's in Ormskirk without ever having even been in the juniors. He has a great big desk, twice as big as anyone elses and it isn't as if he needs a desk at all. He never seems to do any work and Mrs Gibbons seems to let him just sit there. She never shouts at him and I don't really see her talk to him much even. Sometimes he puts his head down on his desk and actually goes to sleep, especially on days like this when the fire's lit and it's so warm in here. There were icicles down the windows when we got here this morning but they've melted now. I could see all sorts of shapes that mum says are Jack Frost's drawings but I'm not sure if he is real. I am sure though that I saw a face behind a drawing of a tree on the window and somebody must have drawn the tree.

Brian's playing with his willy now. He's always doing that but if I give him a dirty look he usually stops.

I've got another problem to worry about today. Mrs Gibbons has marked a sum wrong and I know it's right. I've put 10 take away 6 equals 4 as my answer and it's come back with a big red cross through it. After thinking for as long as I can without Mrs Gibbons noticing that I'm not writing, I've decided to do the sum again, the only way I can, with the "wrong" answer. It's nearly home time now anyway so she'll mark it tonight and probably forget about it by tomorrow.

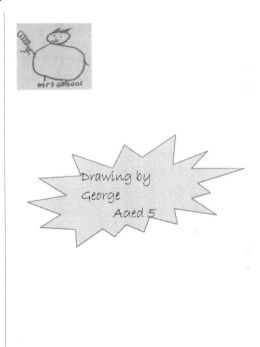

The following morning saw Mrs Gibbons slapping me around the face for my "defiance" in giving the same answer to a sum that had already been marked as "wrong". I was pushed around while I sobbed.

When she had finished venting her anger she sent me to the kitchen to wash my face then followed me out a few minutes later to give me two humbugs, as she begged me not to tell my mum what had happened. I was just relieved that it was over but of course I didn't tell mum - I was too scared to. I didn't want to eat the humbugs either but was scared not to in case Mrs Gibbons found out.

As for the orange box, I grew up with a love of boxes. Not exactly the orange box type, I prefer pretty ones but even a nicely made cardboard box has its merits. China trinket boxes are my favourite for aesthetic reasons, followed by small wooden ones.

With her round brown glasses and her brown, greying, wavy hair parted on one side with a hair clip on the other side, Mrs Gibbons looked, for all intents and purposes like a kindly motherly or grandmotherly figure. Although when I was five she would be just about forty, she seemed older. This would be as much due to the way she acted as well as how she looked. She was far from motherly though. Everything about her was too loud. Her speaking voice was booming and when she shouted the sound seemed to bounce off the walls.

There wasn't much that I could say that I did like about Mrs Gibbons. It would be hard to like somebody who hit children like she did. Corporal punishment was allowed in schools of course, but lines were crossed in her class.

One thing I did like in her class though, was another box, her treasure box. It was small and made out of wood and contained bits of old jewellery which to me were beautiful. We were rewarded for good behaviour or good work, very occasionally, as well as being punished for doing wrong, albeit at times as erratically, which for the girls meant being allowed to choose an item from the box. On the very rare occasions when a boy was considered to have done well then he would be given a humbug from the huge glass jar Mrs Gibbons kept topped up on her desk. I was given the distinct impression by Mrs Gibbons that all boys were lazy. She didn't seem to give them much credit for excelling at anything. I also left the class thinking boys didn't have singing voices because they weren't allowed in the choir, as we were told that only girls could sing.

I was invited to choose something from the treasure box following the time I made Mrs Gibbons cry. I was called in from the playground one dinner time to see her. I groaned, thinking I would be asked to carry out one of my "privileges" - her word for a tidy up job or chore of some sort. Monica had the regular privilege of emptying the tea leaves out of Mrs Gibbons' large tea cup each day at the back of the field in the school grounds. It was when I went in and saw Mrs Gibbons mopping her tears up that my heart was to stand still. It turned out that one of the boys had "snitched" to her that on the way home on the bus the night before, I had called her "Old Ma Gibgobs". We all laughed on the bus and I thought no more of it until this confrontation. It was the scariest moment of my school days when I realised that she knew, as I stood facing her. My heart began to beat normally again as she actually made it easier for me by saying, through the sobs, that it couldn't possibly be true and I didn't so much as have to deny it as to stand there nodding in agreement that I would never be so wicked, while wondering if I could possibly have escaped being thrashed. I did escape and was then rewarded by a now sobbing through the smiles, Mrs Gibbons, as she handed me the box.

Something puzzled me about Mrs Gibbons since my first day at school when I had just turned five and I still do wonder about it. Julie had gone on ahead of me and mum with Gerry and Eddie as mum was accompanying me on the bus. I fell over on the way to the bus stop on the cinder path by the Malayan college, grazing my knee, dirtying my long white socks and getting dirt in the wound. Mum took me home to clean me up and when we arrived at the school an hour later, Mrs Gibbons was standing waiting in the doorway and watched us get off the bus. Julie and the boys wouldn't know what had happened so wouldn't have been able to tell her where we were and why we hadn't arrived at school so I could understand her wondering. What I didn't understand was the way she reacted when we did arrive. She shouted out to Mrs Maybury in the junior class, "She's here, she's here!", as if I was a long lost child, or somebody special. I remember thinking it was good that she seemed to like me a lot but strange that she didn't know me so why should she be so pleased. More than anything I was busy thinking how I could get mum to stay with me as I didn't want her to leave.

The school had first opened its doors on 3 May 1869 to approximately forty children, all housed in the two rooms which made up the building. It wasn't until sixty years later that the third room was added as children from the surrounding areas joined the school. St Kentigern's school in Melling closed in 1945 when St Mary's admitted a further 21 pupils. During my time at the school the three rooms in the single storey building were used as a classroom each for the infants and juniors although prior to St Bede's secondary modern opening towards the end of the 1950s, the children remained at St Mary's until they left school altogether at fifteen, that is unless they passed the eleven plus to go on to grammar school. The third room served a variety of purposes including the kitchen area which had a white Belfast sink on the left hand side, used for washing the dishes, while in the centre of the room stood an old, scrubbed, dull grey looking wooden table. This is where the school dinners were served, having been delivered to the school each day by the Education Authority. The opposite side of the kitchen area had hooks running the length of the wall which is where we hung our coats and the adjoining wall had two wash hand basins, the only ones on the school premises.

On Tuesday afternoons the kitchen area was turned into a gym for the infants class. This transformation involved Mrs Gibbons pushing the table from the centre of the room until it was flush against the wall. We then listened to the "Music and Movement" programme on the radio while we charged round the room like a herd of elephants. We didn't change out of our shoes into pumps and the noise we made was deafening so much so that you could barely hear the radio. If the weather was fine, however, then Mrs Gibbons would open the window and place the radio on the window sill and we would go outside for the lesson.

The infant classroom with its assortment of 30 or so desks squeezed inside, left little room for walking round, even for young children. It looked cosy, if a little odd as a classroom where the coal fire burned in one corner in the winter time, surrounded by a fire guard. The homely ambience was enhanced on Monday mornings when Mrs Gibbons brought her washing in to dry, draped over the fire guard with her oversized, knee length bloomers in full view. On such days you could see the steam dripping down the window by the fireplace, reminding me of mum at home in the kitchen. The fire was also used to dry the knickers of any of the girls who had wet themselves in class, by placing the wet garments to dry on the fire guard without them being rinsed out first. This would be followed by a mop up operation with the mop and bucket which was always standing in readiness in the corner One particular little girl in the class with John had regular "accidents" and each time it happened she was told by Mrs Gibbons that "Kind Johnny would mop it up." The room didn't smell so good on these "accident" days but at other times it was scented with a mixture of the smoke from the coal burning fire, school dinners, crayons, the lavender toilet water Mrs Gibbons used, and humbugs. I don't ever remember any of the boys wetting themselves but maybe they kept quiet about it.

There were usually one or two of the children's drawings on the walls in the classroom, Mrs Gibbons having selected the best drawings for display as the concept of encouragement and praise for effort didn't seem to cross her mind. Apart from the work of the budding Rembrandt's, the walls were adorned with pictures of Our Lady and The Sacred Heart, the huge classroom clock and a crucifix.

After the register had been taken and before the start of lessons each day, there were a couple of daily rituals to be performed, the first of these being to check that we all had a hanky. We had to stand for this, holding up whatever passed for a hanky and long before the days of us using paper tissues, if we ran out of real ones then a piece of rag would do, to the tune of Mrs Gibbons chanting, "Hankies out, hankies in". If you had a hanky you could then sit down but if you didn't, then you were given a few lashes of the ruler across the palm of your hand at some point in the morning. The ruler was the official punishment for the infants, as well as being sent to the "dunces' corner".

We then all had to stand up again to recite the following school prayer. For this we placed our left hand on our stomach and right hand upright from the elbow and when everybody was in position, the right hands would sweep up to start the sign of the cross, in synchrony:-

Little Lamb who made thee?
Dost thou know who made thee?
Gave thee life, and bid thee feed
By the stream and o'er the mead;
Gave thee clothing of delight;
Softest clothing, woolly, bright;
Gave thee such a tender voice,
Making all the vales rejoice?
Little Lamb, who made thee?
Dost thou know who made thee?

Little Lamb, I'll tell thee,
Little Lamb, I'll tell thee:
He is called by thy name,
For he calls himself a Lamb.
He is meek and he is mild;
He became a little child,
I a child and thou a lamb,
We are called by his name.
Little Lamb, God bless thee!
Little Lamb, God bless thee!

William Blake

Such sweet innocence - reciting the prayer each day somehow made me feel special.

The teaching methods of the day were by the three "Rs" which we learnt at our own pace. I enjoyed the learning, which was done by repetition and it worked well for most of us. For reading we had the "Look and say" method using the Beacon Reader Old Lob series of books. Writing was the most repetitive, having to write lines such as, "The cat sat on the mat", over and over, covering several pages, structured to add extra words after so many pages.

As our writing techniques developed we were given compositions to write, or essays as they became known later. When Mrs Gibbons read my first composition, it was the only time I ever made her laugh, in fact I don't remember any other time ever seeing her laugh. I didn't think it was funny though and was very embarrassed. We had been asked to write about a dream we had had and I wrote the true story of one of my own dreams, that it was raining "cats and dogs". I was really proud of my piece of work and as I handed it to Mrs Gibbons I waited eagerly for her reaction which didn't turn out to be as I had expected. She threw her head back and howled laughing at my description of the cats and dogs falling out of the sky, hitting people on their heads on the way down.

Sums were done with the aid of "counters" or small ceramic shells, as used in my ten take away sum mentioned earlier. We then progressed to multiplication, long multiplication and division sums, all by constant repetition, doing the same sums over and over again until they were imprinted on our brains.

In the classroom, Mrs Gibbons spent of lot of her time walking round, watching us, checking that nobody stopped working. You would catch her occasionally gazing out of the window but you always knew she was aware of what you were doing.

When she did sit down behind her own desk she would flop into her chair and surround herself with things to do as though she was restless, randomly picking things up and putting them down again. At other times she would sit on top of her desk facing us with her oversized bloomers again in full view, with the ruler ever on hand ready for anybody who laughed.

Tuesday afternoons were to be looked forward to. We would sit at our desks as usual but with our heads down on our folded arms, listening to a "broadcast" on the wireless after each being given a humbug from Mrs Gibbons' jar. It was peaceful, the only problem being you had to make sure you didn't get too comfortable and fall asleep, otherwise you were quite likely to get a rude awakening from Mrs Gibbons if she was in a bad mood.

Nature study lessons took place about twice a year when we were taken out to walk round the school grounds to look at the wild flowers growing, worms, birds and any other form of life outside. These little jaunts outside usually followed Mrs Gibbons asking the class to remind her of the last time we had a "nature study" lesson. When some of us didn't know what she was talking about as we had never had a nature study lesson, she would then usher us outside for half an hour.

The infants class was also where we were first introduced to God. Not that we didn't hear about Him at home from mum and dad and the older ones, but it was at school where we were indoctrinated into the catholic faith as well having the horrors of sin spelt out to us.

I remember being taught about the two categories of sin. A venial sin being the less serious of the two evils, the other being mortal sin, which if committed, could be punished by God by burning in hell fire for eternity if you didn't confess, in the confessional. Confession is made directly to God through the medium of a priest. At this early stage we were preparing to take the sacraments of confession and Holy Communion and it was once we had made our first confession and first Holy Communion when we were just turned seven, that we would be punished for our sins. We were also taught never to forget that a sin could be committed by "thought, word or deed" so you could burn in hell if you hadn't even done anything wrong, just thought about it.

Mrs Gibbons once demonstrated the effects of sin on the soul by drawing a picture on the blackboard of a white dress. She asked us for examples of sin, a popular one being the killing of worms or pulling the legs off a daddy long legs. For each sin called out, she would make a black mark on the board by licking her finger and wiping some of the chalk off the dress. Each time you sinned, a bit more of your soul would be blackened until it eventually wore away if you committed too many sins. I had a terrifying nightmare one night after one of these lessons.

Once we had taken our first sacraments, missing mass on a Sunday or Holy Day of Obligation was a mortal sin and had to be confessed, otherwise if you were taken ill or had an accident and died suddenly then you would go straight to hell. It was explained, however, that if you just happened to be on your way to confession when you died, then your soul would be redeemed and you would be forgiven and go to heaven, although you might have to spend some time in purgatory first. We lapped all of this up of course, believing every word. To summarise, mortal sins always need to be confessed or it's hell and damnation for your soul when you die, whereas it is in your own interest to confess and do penance for the venial sins to give yourself a chance of a better afterlife by entering into heaven more quickly. If, however, you were to die without having confessed and done penance for your venial sins, then you would need to spend some time in purgatory, to purge your soul of your sins, before you get to heaven. The length of time you would spend in purgatory would depend on how long it took to cleanse your soul but entry into heaven could be helped by the prayers of the faithful and indeed we said another prayer every morning, in the junior class for the repose of a soul in purgatory.

A third place in the afterlife is limbo which we were taught is a place for the soul of any person who has not been baptised and therefore still bears the original sin. This includes any new born baby that dies shortly after birth without having been baptised as we are all born in a state of sin from the original sin. We were told that if it was known a new born baby's life was in imminent danger then anybody could baptise them with any water available, otherwise the baby's soul would remain in limbo until the end of the world. This belief is still held by many Catholics today and if I am completely honest, I would have to go along with a baptism in such circumstances.

We were each given a copy of The Catechism for which we paid one penny The catechism is a written Code of Behaviour for catholic children. The following is an extract from the catechism, from memory:-

Who made you?
God made me.

How did God make you?
God made me in his own image and likeness.

Why did God make you?
God made me to love, honour and obey him.

We were also given a copy of the Bible Narrative, at a cost of threepence in pre decimal money. This contained stories from the bible and must be where I learned as much as I remember from the bible, along with whatever else I was taught in religious lessons. I am amazed at how many of the parables I do remember, considering I haven't looked much at The Bible since I left school.

At twelve o'clock promptly each day, we stopped working as along with Catholics around the world, we stood to say The Angelus, a prayer in celebration of the annunciation to Mary of her imminent immaculate conception.

We then stayed at our desks to eat our dinner after placing a white square "dinner cloth" over the desk. The cloths were also delivered to the school and changed for a freshly laundered one each Monday morning. If you didn't keep an eye on your cloth you could well find a dirty one in your desk at some point on a Wednesday morning, bearing the same stains as one used by one of the boys on Monday and Tuesday. The dinners were served by two lovely dinner ladies, Mrs Bates (whom most of us went through the school mistakenly calling "Mrs Bakes"), and Mrs Valentine. Those of us who didn't have a hot dinner brought a packed lunch. Most of us loved the hot dinners but our family had them in the winter time and brought sandwiches for the rest of the year. We would have been entitled to free school meals but mum and dad wouldn't have allowed that for which I am eternally grateful, as I believed at the time that we would have been the only children in the school to have free dinners.

Playtime was spent in the two tarmacked areas used by both the girls and boys but the smaller ground was used mostly by the boys for football while the girls played skipping and ball games in the other. Some of our other playground games can still be seen being played today, such as "What's the time Mr Wolf?", all passed down to us from our mothers and grandmothers.

At the age of seven we graduated to the junior class to be taught by Mrs Maybury, who like Mrs

Gibbons, was a war widow but she bore no resemblance to Mrs Gibbons in any other way. She wore her snowy white hair tied back in a bun every day. Mum said the story was that her hair had turned white suddenly when she was given the news of her husband's death during the war but I don't know the truth of that. There was no denying the pure whiteness of her hair though and she, like Mrs Gibbons, couldn't have been aged much more than about forty at the time. She was slightly built, very slim and had bright blue eyes. She wore bright red lipstick which she would reapply after lunch each day and then dab it with an embroidered hanky, which again she always had, tucked inside her sleeve. The red lipstick was in stark contrast to the very pale, almost white face powder she wore which could have given her a gothic look if she had dressed differently. She wore a skirt, blouse buttoned to the neck, fastened with a cameo broach, all covered by a cardigan. Mrs Maybury was refined and ladylike at all times.

Our days with Mrs Maybury would start with the following hymn:-

> Little king so fair and sweet
> See us gathered round thy feet
> Be thou monarch of our school
> It shall prosper 'neath thy rule.
> We will be thy subjects true
> Brave to suffer brave to do
> All our hearts to thee we bring
> Take them, keep them, little king

As we recited the words in parrot fashion, I had no doubt that we were talking to Jesus even though I never paid much attention to the meaning. I'm not sure if I knew what "monarch" meant while Monica says she thought it had something to do with her.

Amongst other hymns and prayers we learned the Lords' Prayer and the Hail Mary. We were of course told how Mary, Our Lady, was the mother of Jesus and also that she was a mother in heaven, to every child. We were told to pray to God through Mary as she would pass our prayers on. I found it a comfort as a child, believing I had some sort of direct contact with heaven. One day when I was seven and having a bad day in school I stood in the playground, looked up to the sky and told Mary that I had four years left in the school, which was a very long time so could she please ask God to make it a bit better for me. Whatever my problem had been that day it blew over but through the years when I've had bad days, there have been many more times I have called on Mary.

Punishment from Mrs Maybury was a few strokes across your hand with an eight inch strip of leather, we called "the strap". This was the only punishment we had in her class as she never lost control by lashing out at the children and if ever she knew what went on in the infants' class, then she must have turned a blind eye.

We were graded for our lessons as there were thirty of us in the class with ages ranging from seven to eleven. The classroom was more spacious than the infants class with desks lined up into three rows with each row constituting a grade where the ages could overlap depending on progress and ability.

We were taught in the juniors how to do double or "cursive writing". My writing always looked a mess no matter how hard I tried. Mrs Maybury said it looked like a spider had crawled out of the inkwell across the page. We didn't have fountain pens to start with so had to dip our pen nibs into the inkwell, positioned at the top corner of our desks. We then used blotting paper to mop up the residue but if we splashed ink onto the page there was nothing we could do about the mess. If the splash landed on a word, you had to rewrite it on top of the mark. Consequently, my work often looked very messy. Writing was much easier when we graduated to filling fountain pens from the inkwells but we had to make sure the pen nib wasn't too wide or else the result was a dreadful mess. We eventually progressed to using cartridge pens which sorted out some of the problems, apart from handwriting styles.

For subjects such as geography, history or religion we would be given passages to learn for homework of a whole page from a text book, to be written out from memory the following morning. I loved the challenge of learning the lines which I could soak up at that age just by reciting an extra line after each read through.

Weekly spelling tests again posed no problem for me or most of the children to some degree or other. There was one boy in our class, however, who got almost all the spellings wrong every week for which he was given the strap. His name was Paul and I remember some of the children laughing at him one day when he was asked by Mrs Maybury the date of Christmas Day and he didn't know. This puzzled me. To speak to and to play with, Paul was as bright and intelligent as any other child, if not more so and it remained a puzzle to me as to why he simply couldn't spell. Then years later when I understood how not all children learn in the same way, as with Dyslexia, I began to understand.

Something else about Paul has puzzled me since I was ten as I've been debating with myself ever since as to whether or not he saved my life. I don't remember the reason why, but for a short spell, the bus to Waddicar Lane in Melling was diverted, and we had to get off somewhere down near the canal and cross the bridge to finish the walk home from school. Just as I was stepping onto the bridge one night, some bright spark thought it was a good idea to swing the bridge as I had one foot on the bridge and one on the canal bank. Paul quickly ran towards me, grabbed my arm and pulled me to safety onto the bank. I couldn't swim and am sure I would have fallen into the water if he hadn't pulled me away as there was nothing to hold onto and, well, I may not be here to tell the tale if Paul hadn't pulled me away.

By this time we were all well aware of how to get to stay out of hell and to get to heaven, and our religious teaching continued as a high priority, naturally, with the Ten Commandments being reinforced as well as reading and learning more passages from the bible, which was something else I enjoyed very much.

Mrs Maybury would open a notebook each Friday morning to tick our names off as she collected a penny off each of us, after collecting the dinner money. The pennies were for what we called the "Probagation" short for Propagation of the Faith. I didn't have a clue at the time what the word meant but it sounded impressive and I was given my penny each week by mum.

For non academic lessons, the girls were given tray cloths and altar cloths to embroider and we were also taught to knit while the boys played with Mecanno. I never could knit neatly, my stitches were big, loose and uneven because I was in too much of a hurry. Embroidery involved stitching over very pretty flower outlines by either a satin stitch which covered a petal on the pattern with a series of flat stitches, giving a professional finish which took ages to do, or alternatively a chain stitch which covered the outside of the petal with two simple stitches. For months during our sewing lessons Mrs Maybury had me as the only girl doing satin stitch as the others raced through their work with the chain stitch. Eventually I plucked up the courage to ask her why this was. She told me that she asked me to do it as I was the only one she thought had enough patience. I couldn't have agreed less but of course couldn't say so, as I just had to get on with it, thinking how she had seen my knitting which was like a rag, my handwriting she said looked like a spider had crawled across the page, so I couldn't imagine how she thought I was patient. Looking back now, I think that maybe what she did see was not so much patience as perseverance and an ability to see things through, which is something I would go along with - having heard the expression, "like a dog at a bone" used about myself so many times that I have to believe it.

We continued to eat our dinner at our desks in the juniors with a beaker of water we were given each day. We were all used to drinking water, as lemonade and cordials were only ever for Christmas and special occasions and most of the children were happy with the water, having already had the bottle of milk issued to us each morning. The children of the licensee of the Derby Arms pub along the road, past the church, attended the school and one of the boys, Bernard, brought cordial to drink every day which he would share with one or two of his friends. I would watch, wondering what the cordial tasted like and Bernard would sometimes ask me if I wanted some then laugh with his friends and say I couldn't have any. Then one day he poured some into a beaker and handed it to me. I thanked him, thinking he wasn't so bad after all. That just shows how gullible I was. He watched with his friends as I took a sip from the beaker. The drink tasted disgusting and it was all I could do not to spit it out. I told Bernard they were selling some horrible stuff in their pub and couldn't understand how the boys liked it so much. It was years before the penny dropped and I realised that the drink had been doctored - I dread to think what with.

Once a week Mrs Maybury would give us permission to draw in half a page of our "private work books" - a blue exercise book with lined paper. We would have a good half hour to spend drawing and it didn't take long to fill half a page so I regularly extended mine to a full page or even two. I was never caught but then believed Mrs Maybury respected our privacy and didn't check the books. This belief was confirmed when I saw one boy and girl drawing diagrams in their books each week with graphic descriptions of how babies were made.

At the end of each day, those of us who travelled on the bus would have to line up and walk, "single file" out to the bus stop, in silence. If anybody either spoke or ran then they would be dealt with the next day by getting the strap for "bad behaviour yesterday evening". Then all hell would let loose once we were on the bus and out of sight.

Mrs Maybury took politeness and genteel behaviour to extremes at times as on the occasion of a Christmas party when I forgot myself and laughed at something. She told me to stop laughing and being silly.

St Mary's School - Redeveloped (2012)

Chapter Six

St Mary's - The brighter side

Having said all I have about St Mary's, in many ways it was idyllic. Tucked away on Prescot Road we could have been deep in the countryside, as even without a hill in sight, we were surrounded by fields and farms, a row of houses along Cunscough Lane and the village church of St Mary's which was built in the year 1798 and still stands today. And all just three miles from Kirkby.

The majority of the children at the school were from the surrounding farms and cottages along Cunscough Lane, just across the field next to the school grounds as well as one or two from the houses on Prescot Road. Then there were the Melling children who travelled on the bus with us, and those who joined us en route, such as the Donovan brothers who attended St Mary's for a brief spell in between private schools, wearing purple blazers from their previous school when none of the rest of us wore a uniform. There were also a couple of other families from Kirkby such as the McMahons and the Lavins. The village of Bickerstaffe was within the catchment area of the school as although it is about three miles away in a different direction from Kirkby, this was the closest Catholic primary school serving that area. The Bickerstaffe children travelled to school in style by taxi as they weren't on any bus route.

Some of the names of the other families from the school as far as I remember were Hurst, Johnson, Bullen, Tyrer, Swift, Weston, Norris, Harris, Culley, Coyne, Neary, Fazakerley, Harvey, Corsini, Starkey, Rigby, Smith, Williams, Spencer, Cheetham, Griffiths, Tighe and Daly. The Harris girls were amazing to see. There were seven girls in the family who were all sent to school looking absolutely immaculate and beautifully dressed in dresses knitted by Mrs Harris. The youngest child was a boy, Michael.

The school closed after just over one hundred years, to be renovated and reopened as The Chesterfield Restaurant which in turn has now ceased trading as a restaurant and at the time of writing I am told has been granted planning permission to be renovated as a bungalow. The Hen and Chickens pub which was just a bit further down the road, across Cunscough Lane, recently closed and re-opened as an Indian restaurant. In the other direction the Derby Arms pub is still open. As far as I know, the school had been purpose built, in the same grounds as the cottage where the Norris family lived, although the original house has now been rebuilt.

Julie, as the eldest, had been the first to go to school, to Holy Name, about three miles away in Fazakerley. She was joined a year and a half later by Gerry and then Eddie, for a short spell of about six months. Mum and dad were not happy with the progress they were making at Holy Name as dad said they were learning too much about God and not enough of anything else, so they took the Ribble bus out to Prescot Road to visit St Mary's, the picturesque little village school set amongst the farmland, where they met Mrs Maybury and it was agreed that the children could transfer schools. I followed Eddie three years later, to be joined by the others in steady succession, ending with Sheila.

The journey to St Mary's involved catching the bus in Waddicar Lane in Melling. It was just over two miles away from home with one disadvantage being that it was too far to walk and the buses only ran once an hour. Although Holy Name was a similar distance away from home, the Corporation buses were more frequent. One of the older girls on the estate, Pat Bradley, accompanied Julie to school on the bus to Holy Name each day. Julie got to know the route so well that after attending the school for a few months, at the age of five she decided she wanted to go home one day and without telling anyone, walked out of school and walked home, causing mum to think she was seeing things when Julie walked in the house on her own.

The Ribble bus stop was placed handily outside the Post Office in Waddicar Lane which also stocked groceries and sweets, and this is where we spent some of our pocket money on Friday mornings. The range of sweets included sherbet lemons, pear drops and pineapple chunks to name a few, all sold by the ounce from big glass jars stacked high on the shelves. These "boiled" sweets, rich in sugar, were boiled as hard as bullets to be weighed out and sold in quantities of either two ounces or a quarter pound. The good old penny gobstopper must have a mention. It was so big I can't imagine ever giving one to a child but at the time, we loved them, partly because of how long they lasted as well as how they changed colour the smaller they got so you could take it out of your mouth to check the colour at regular intervals. There was a smaller version of the gobstopper sold for a halfpenny. Jelly babies were not much different to today's variety apart from the black ones which were rare, so if you did get a black one you would have to make it last as long you possibly could, to make the most of it or else trade it for two of a different colour.

The proprietors of the Post Office, Mr and Mrs Percival, were very patient as we stood for ages choosing what to buy and asking the price of the sweets. There was one boy who never lived down with the rest of us the day he asked the price of a penny arrow bar one morning while we queued up behind him.

There were business premises next to the Post Office with a wooden plank across the entrance to the driveway. During the long, icy winters of our childhood, this piece of wood made an excellent slide to skate across as we waited for the bus. It would be about two feet wide, covering the width of the driveway of about ten feet and as the weeks went by we had it as smooth as a piece of glass, of course never giving a thought to any pedestrian crossing it or indeed the wheels of a vehicle. The last time I slid across I fell and banged by head and was rendered unconscious and had to go home. I never plucked up the courage to have another go.

On arriving at school we could play in the playground until the bell was rung - pretty much the same routine as today apart from the fact that there was never a parent in sight other than on a child's first day at school.

We had a brick built air raid shelter, another remnant of the war, in the school playground. The shelter was about 30 feet long, open at each end and out of bounds to the children as far as the teachers were concerned. All it took for the boys to gain entry was to deliberately throw a ball in and be given permission to go into the shelter to retrieve it. They would then come out saying the shelter was piled high with skeletons and I wasn't the only one to believe them. I never went into the shelter myself, as hard as I tried not to let the boys see they could do something the girls couldn't, skeletons were something I wasn't prepared to deal with. There was also an old well in the grounds which never looked very safe. Luckily, apart from throwing stones and rubbish into the chamber, it didn't hold much interest so we kept away from it.

Even though this period was only ten to fifteen years or so after the war, that was something which never seemed to be talked about much when I was growing up and to me, although the war was something my family had experienced, as it was before I was born, the word "war" was just that, a word, or a part of history. I don't ever remember a teacher talking about either of the world wars.

While some people must still have been dealing with their losses and tragedies, others were able to put it all behind them and look to the future. Our family came out of the war unscathed with mum relating tales of rationing and shortages which did make interesting stories of life in "the olden days" to me. She talked about how her father kept the better cigarettes for his regular customers with passing shoppers being sold the less popular "Camel" brand which apparently had a bad taste. Apart from these stories I was never aware of how people suffered until I was a lot older.

The word "afford" was one I heard a lot of throughout my school days. Of course it is a word we all use but when I was at school it was more often prefixed with the word "can't" in relation to our family. I once heard a girl talking to her brother about something we couldn't afford like them because we were poor. She was right of course but what she said couldn't be beaten to make you feel small.

Peer pressure is hard on children and if they have a dad like we had then it's even harder. Not having the latest styles is one thing but being given, or even forced to wear an alternative from a bygone age is a totally different matter. Dad's answer every time to complaints about not having the same things as our peers was that we weren't sheep and didn't have to be the same as everyone else. There were times I would have rather been a sheep. A typical example is the story Julie tells of how she once needed a pair of Wellington boots to wear to school after a heavy snowfall. Mrs Maybury had said the children could play in the playground as long as they had a pair, so Julie went home to be reassured by Dad who told her it wouldn't be a problem, she would be out in the snow soon as he would pick a pair up for her the following day. Wellies were and still are readily available and inexpensive so Julie waited excitedly for dad to come home from work the following day so she could play in the snow. He kept to his word and produced a brown paper parcel. You wouldn't have thought you could go wrong asking for a pair of Wellington boots but when Julie opened up the parcel, instead of seeing the standard black boots, she saw cowboy boots, brown ones, complete with pictures of cowboy hats and spurs down the sides. Her cries and protests went unheeded as she was sent to school in the cowboy boots the next morning.

Amongst the "idyllic" qualities of the school were Wednesday mornings when we all went to mass at 8 o'clock at St Mary's church, where Father Greer, the parish priest, would say the mass. This meant leaving home an hour earlier to arrive at school in time to all walk down to the church together. When we arrived back at school the dinner ladies would serve us steaming hot, milky cocoa which would taste delicious, especially on a cold winter morning.

The most idyllic days of school for me by far, were during the month of May which we dedicated to Our Lady. At the beginning of the month we made an altar by placing one of the tray cloths we had embroidered on top of a book case. We then added a statue of Mary, some night light candles to be burned throughout the day and best of all, we picked wild flowers from the surrounding fields, to be placed on the altar. Having no doubts about Our Lady in heaven, this to me was magical.

St Mary's Chapel - 2012

On a Sunday afternoon during May we had our May procession at the church. The girls all wore a white dress and veil with two of us being chosen each year to be "strewers", leading the other children in procession round the church, scattering flower petals from a basket they carried while singing hymns such as "Bring flowers of the rarest" and "I'll sing a hymn to Mary." This was followed by a second procession in July in celebration of the month of the Sacred Heart.

The school toilets were housed in a brick built shed

behind the school but the word "toilet" was taboo at St Mary's. This was something we never questioned, accepting that it was considered impolite to use the word and although I had heard of more genteel sounding names such as ladies, gents or lavatory, we weren't allowed to use those names either. The school had its own name; if we needed to ask during lesson times to go to the toilet we had to ask, "Please Mrs Gibbons/Maybury, may I go to the places?"

The places themselves were far from genteel as they were glorified buckets, like a beer barrel. A council van turned up fortnightly to exchange the full buckets for empty ones. We had one for the girls, one for the boys and a third for the teachers, all housed in a brick built hut situated in the school grounds with partitions between each "place". With the only wash hand basins being the ones in the kitchen, I don't remember us being encouraged to wash our hands as we had to hurry back to class.

The good things about the school were of course, overshadowed by the overly strict discipline doled out by the teachers, especially Mrs Gibbons but we did cope and accept things as they were. It certainly made some of us behave. The teachers may have had their favourites but they did generally treat us equally in that even Mrs Gibbons' pets weren't spared a belting if they misbehaved on one of her bad days.

Mrs Maybury's leaving present to Monica

Ten years after leaving St Mary's, Monica, as a newly qualified teacher, was sitting in the staff room on her first tea break at her first teaching post, being regaled with stories of the teacher whose place she had just taken, following retirement. The more she was told about this teacher, such as her first name and where she lived, quite apart from the idiosyncrasies, the louder a bell rang. It transpired that Mrs Gibbons had changed her name as she had remarried and Monica had now taken her place.

Chapter Seven

Notre Dame Collegiate School

It was my first day back to school today after the summer holidays and I'm now in the second year at Notre Dame Collegiate in Everton Valley, which I've heard said is the second highest ranking girls' grammar school in Liverpool. We have three classes to each year which are streamed as form, middle and upper and I'm in the middle, still, which surprises me after my performance last year.

My new exercise books are set out neatly on the rug in front of me, ready to be backed with the assortment of odds and ends of wallpaper dad has found for me. I have my eye on a big, pink cabbage rose pattern which will fit nicely on the front of my French verb book as it's half the size of the others. Dad's trying to help by asking me about my new timetable and saying how interesting it sounds and I know he means well but it isn't working. This is in between him talking to Harold Wilson on the television and I won't repeat what he's just called him but will say there's a blob of Welsh rarebit dripping down the screen. Dad has this treat for his supper most nights, prepared to his strict instructions by mum only, as he says she gets the balance of cheese and milk just right. I'm not sure why it matters so much, the amount of times it ends up down the screen. I'm moving my books out of the way, just in case.

I feel guilty about school because I feel like I let mum and dad down last year but the truth of the matter is that I'm very unhappy there. The thought of the year ahead is daunting and however pretty my books look on the outside will have no bearing on how I fill them.

Before I first started last year, I hadn't given any thought to the difference between the village school of St Mary's where everybody knew each other and where my siblings were, to this school in the centre of Liverpool where I wouldn't know a soul and I found it hard, especially as I had never known what it was like to feel as if you are on your own. Most of the girls seemed to know at least one person from their old school and they hang around together in little cliques. By the time I walked out of school on the last day of term at the Christmas break, I had made my mind up that I wasn't going back. All that was needed was for me to pick the right moment to tell dad. Somehow I thought mum would be easier to get round so I wasn't worried about her but dad was a different proposition.

I sat on my bed one afternoon and waited for him to come home from work while I practised what to say. He walked in and I heard him chatting happily so I braced myself and seized the moment to make my announcement as I walked downstairs and told both mum and dad that I had decided not to go back to Everton Valley but would be joining my friends at St Bede's after Christmas. They took it very well on the whole, sitting me down to tell me what most girls would give for a place in the school and how I would soon settle down. My protests that "They can have my place" went unheeded as it became clear that I had to return.

My prayers to St Jude, the patron saint of hopeless causes, for the school to burn down, went unanswered as the building is still standing today.

I did settle down at school, after a fashion, but it wasn't in a good way. During the first week back after that first Christmas, at dinner time one day, a few of the girls from my class were playing around, jumping down a set of stone steps just outside the school doorway. I joined in and found myself laughing for the first time since I started the school. These girls didn't seem as serious as some of the others and it turned out that the four of them, Christine, Ann, Margaret and Linda, were all from different schools and were just getting to know one another. They became my new friends which was good in some ways as I was a lot happier but it was also my undoing as that was the day I realised I could have fun but it came at the expense of my education as from then on, I did as little school work as I could get away with. There was nobody around any more to give me a slap if I did wrong or indeed to even tell me off, as there was an almost total lack of monitoring in the school. The pupils were never accountable individually to the Education Authority for their performance and so it was easy to slip through the system unnoticed. If we were caught misbehaving in class we were made to stand outside the classroom for the duration of the lesson. I never liked this as I was always worried in case I was seen by Sister Dolores, our history teacher, or her friend, Sister Julie who did catch me once and told me she'd heard all about me from Sister Dolores. That came as a bit of shock because although I disliked Sister Dolores immensely, I didn't know I could be the subject of discussion between the two of them and found it a bit unnerving. I realise now it was because I wasn't working but I wish they had asked me why and that I would have been able to answer them. At other times we could be sent to Sister Francis, the headmistress, for a telling off which always embarrassed me because I knew I had been stupid and wouldn't know how to explain myself. I may have been embarrassed but was never given any other reason to worry as all that ever happened would be for Sister to ask me what I had done, confirm with me that I wouldn't do it again and then ask after mum who she seemed to have taken a liking to.

It was very wrong of Mrs Gibbons to hit us but I believe she was just very highly strung and didn't bear any malice, which was more than I believed of some of the teachers at Notre Dame. Not that all the teachers were the same of course, as some were lovely, like Sister Cecilia who had retired and would sit in to cover for an absent teacher. She busied herself helping out, by visiting the classrooms to deliver messages from Sister Francis, or to pass on bits of information such as the time she called round all the classes to show as many of us as she could that there was a rainbow in the sky, before it disappeared. Another day, as we were on our way to the dining hall she called me out of the line to give me a holy picture. I had to pretend like the other girls that I thought it was funny, but secretly I was very touched. If all the teachers had been kind and had spoken to to us like Sister Cecilia, it would definitely have made such a difference.

As with Sister Cecilia, any of the sisters who had retired from teaching kept their involvement with the school, as did Sister Catherine who we would see and hear regularly scuttling along the corridors rattling an old tin which had previously contained tea leaves but now contained coins. Sister Catherine sold raffle tickets continuously and became known throughout the school as "Sister Flog It".

I could put the rest of the teachers into fairly distinct categories of those who gained respect by teaching us well, while remaining fair and holding our attention; those who were bullies; and those who were nervous wrecks and didn't fare very well, as in the following examples.

I've already mentioned Sister Dolores, the history teacher. I endured the lessons, listening to her roaring like a lion, spitting as she spoke, putting me in mind of a steam train. Her voice could have been in competition with the fans at Goodison Park just around the corner, if an Everton match happened to be playing. I know she could be pleasant because I had seen her talking nicely to some of the girls, like Helen, whose dad was a doctor, rather than a docker like some of our dads. That was another thing about the school - it's snobbery. Some of the teachers, such as Sister

Dolores asked nosy questions like where we lived and what our dads did for a living. When asked, I told Sister Dolores I lived in Kirkby. She considered this for a moment before saying, "I see". I understood from that that she was seeing beyond the eleven year old girl standing in front of her, looking outwardly like the rest of the class.

Miss Diamond, (Dilly to us) taught Latin. While the nuns wore their habits, most of the other teachers had their own unofficial uniform consisting of a brownish or grey tweed suit over a well buttoned up blouse, firmly closed at the neck with a broach. Lisle stockings and brown brogue shoes completed the ensemble. That's how Dilly dressed and with her grey hair brushed severely back from her face, her appearance belied her soft nature and sense of humour. I enjoyed the Latin lessons which came to an end after that first year, as the subject was taught merely to help us with word derivation. The lessons did impress me by teaching me how to break down words and understand new ones with a simple translation from Latin. I wasn't too sure about Dilly when I first met her after she told me off for not doing my homework which of course she had every right to do. Resenting being told off, I went home and prayed that she would die then when she was off school the following day I felt dreadful. I confessed to Julie what I had done but she laughed and told me not to worry, I wouldn't have killed her. All went well after that as Dilly and I got on fine for the rest of the year.

The Furlong sisters, Skinny and Fatty, taught French

and general science respectively. They both wore the lay teachers' uniform but were different in every other way. Skinny Furlong was strict as well as being very pleasant and funny in a sarcastic kind of way. She always sounded enthusiastic which did rub off on to me to help liven up her lessons and help keep my interest.

Her sister was of the nervous type, making it easy to mess around in her class, although I did love the science lessons we had that year. It came as a big disappointment to me to learn that general science was also only taught in the first year and that our science subject from then on was to be biology. That fact added to my dislike of the school, as preparing and lighting a Bunsen Burner had been one of the highlights of school in my first year. I sat through the biology lessons with an almost complete lack of interest, mainly as we seemed to cover more plant life than any living creature, including humans although my most memorable biology lesson was being asked to draw a picture of a stickleback. Although the subject matter was limited, I was quite pleased with my effort but when it came back from marking the only comment the teacher had made was that it would have looked better in colour. A couple of words of encouragement could have gone a long way there.

Miss McLean took us for French from the third year up. She was another one to put the fear of God into me but as I liked the subject I didn't do too badly. In fact I'm amazed at how much French I still remember from my school days.

Sister Julie, who I mentioned earlier after she saw me standing outside the class, sat in for Sister Dolores occasionally, making my heart sink. She didn't do anything apart from sitting looking scary and as she never checked what we were doing, my time was wasted, daydreaming.

For music we had Miss Humphreys who I could liken to pretty as she would liken my voice to tune. She is one of the very few people I have ever completely and utterly disliked. For our first ever music lesson we were asked to stand at the piano in turn to sing a song of Miss Humphreys' choice. I'd never sung on my own before in front of other people and was very nervous, without any confidence in my singing voice. When my turn came I didn't think I sounded too bad but Miss Humphreys didn't agree and said, "I thought you would be able to sing but you're useless, go and sit down". One of the girls in our class, Angela, could sing like an angel. When it came to her turn at the piano she sang *Over the Rainbow*, beautifully. Angela's mum had been a singer and I know she had discussions with the school about possible voice training for Angela but it was decided not to go ahead with it, as it would detract from her school work, which I thought was a waste.

Our English teacher for the first two years was Miss Hughes. I liked her as she was always pleasant and I enjoyed the English lessons. She once confiscated a poem being passed round the class, penned by Christine, with the first line reading, "*Our English teacher is Miss Hughes.*" After reading it she smiled and said to Christine, "I hope your talents won't we wasted." That sticks in my memory as one of the rare occasions when a teacher ever engaged with us on anything bordering a personal level. Something else I have never forgotten happened during one of our English lessons with Miss Hughes. It was the last lesson in the morning when we all stood to say the Angelus at 12 o'clock, before going into the dining hall. As Miss Hughes stood in front of the class on the podium, with her eyes closed and her hands joined in prayer, she wet herself. We continued with the prayer as though nothing had happened and so did she, then she walked out of the room with her head held high. I can only imagine how she felt, where she went to and what she did once we were out of sight but more than anything, I wonder why she didn't run to the toilet at the end of the corridor. Luckily for Miss Hughes, this happened after the poem had been written.

Each school day started with a morning assembly in the hall, attended by the whole school. Apart from the usual prayers and daily hymn, the assembly was to inform us of any forthcoming events in the school and the school prefects, made up of all of the upper sixth form, would report to Sister Francis any misdemeanors of the girls, such as being caught on the way to or from school while not wearing the uniform hat. The school hats were a dark blue felt, shaped like a pudding basin, for winter wear and a straw boater with a dark blue band round it in the summer. The pudding basin hats were an embarrassment, the likes of which were never seen in a Kirkby school so I was always glad to disappear down Whitefield Drive on the bus in the mornings. I secretly loved the boater though, and would have happily worn mine all the time but I had to pretend not to like it in front of my friends. The punishment for not wearing a hat was either to stand on your chair throughout the assembly or to wear it round school for the whole day.

The walls of the hall were lined with the Honours Boards inscribed with the names of past pupils who had graduated from university, including the names of some of our teachers. The dark brown wooden plaques with gold lettering were often pointed out to us as our inspiration as we said a prayer for those named on the boards. Unfortunately, I didn't feel inspired. I found it a bit creepy looking at the names of the dead people and of the names I recognised amongst my teachers, there was nobody who I aspired to be like.

I have read reviews of the school from past pupils, extolling the virtues of some of the teachers and how inspirational they were. Monica did very well at the school, despite not particularly liking it, but all I can say is, the school didn't work for me and vice versa.

Notre Dame Collegiate - it sounds very grand as indeed it was, from the school building itself down to the polish on the floors as well as the beautiful chapel inside the sisters' living quarters which looked quite luxurious to me when glimpsed on the way to the chapel.

I only ever visited the nuns' quarters to attend mass in the chapel, apart from once when I joined the Legion of Mary with my group of friends. Passing through, I caught glimpses of the plush, pale blue fitted carpets throughout the huge rooms and corridors with highly polished furniture, smelling of lavender. Joining the Legion was something we had debated amongst ourselves for some time as although it wasn't really our sort of thing, it meant we could stay indoors legitimately once a week at dinner time instead of having to dodge the teachers as we lurked inside the building, hiding in a broom cupboard whenever we heard footsteps approaching. We were also given a tiny badge as members of the Legion, which was quite pretty. As it happened, we only ever went to a meeting in the chapel once, because we were expelled and sent out for laughing at the teachers' hats.

We said goodbye to Sister Dolores from the third year onwards but my joy was short lived when I met Miss Latham. I really didn't like her, a feeling which was mutual. She reminded me of the pictures I'd seen of Queen Elizabeth I, only in a masculine form - in fact some of us wondered if she was a man. I endured the history lessons but didn't learn very much.

After a brief spell of being taught by a Scottish lady, Mrs McDonald, who wasn't at the school for very long, another Sister Julie, who was also Scottish, took over our geography lessons. I don't know why Mrs McDonald left so suddenly but she too seemed nervous. She once announced at the start of a lesson that anybody who was not prepared to behave should go and sit in the back row. Twenty nine of us crammed into the back row, leaving Christine, who could be a bit of a swot at times, sitting on her own in the front row with tears streaming down her face as she laughed.

I liked Sister Julie who was always bright and cheerful. We had a single and a double lesson for geography each week and while in the third year, we were set a project to be worked on for the whole of half a term, having chosen our topic from a comprehensive list of subjects. My choice from the list was the subject of "oranges". We were to work on our project during the double lesson which we spent in the geography room at the top of the school as well as being our geography homework for the whole of the project. I don't know what Sister Julie did herself during the lessons but she allowed us to get on with our work without ever checking what we were doing, so I took the opportunity to work on my Beatles project instead of the topic of oranges. I had built up an amazing scrap book full of photographs and newspaper cuttings which fitted nicely into my Atlas of the World as I joined in with the rest of the class, singing the Beatles songs, up in the geography room, which we reached by climbing a spiral staircase to the top of the old building which in itself felt like escaping.

These were exciting times during which we revelled in being part of Liverpool, feeling proud and privileged to belong to the city which had been firmly placed on the world map, courtesy of the Beatles, Gerry and the Pacemakers, the Swinging Blue Jeans and Cilla Black, to name a few of the very many singers producing the "Mersey Sound". Sister Julie would smile as we sang and say in her Scottish brogue, "I don't mind you singing girls, as long as you are working".

It didn't bother me that before long I would be asked to produce my project on oranges. My philosophy at the time was to deal with a problem when it presented itself and not to anticipate it before it arrived. Then six weeks later it was time to hand in our written work. When asked for mine I just looked up and said that I didn't have anything. I really don't know now how I had the nerve. Sister Julie's expression changed to something I had never seen on her face before - anger - but still I didn't worry. Instead, I started to laugh, uncontrollably with silly girlish giggles, which set most of the rest of the class off. By this time Sister Julie looked fit to explode as her face changed colour and her voice shook with rage as she told me to stand in front of the class and tell everybody, as I hadn't put anything in writing, all that I had learnt about my chosen topic of oranges.

It took me a while to compose myself but eventually, between the convulsions of laughter, standing in front of the class, I managed to speak, to say that oranges grew on trees. There were no reprisals and I was allowed to get away with it. Mum and dad were never told what I had done although I suspect it may have got back to Sister Francis.

Losing all motivation in school was totally out of character from the little girl I had been at St Mary's where I worked so hard, taking pride in and excelling in my work. I never stopped being polite and respectful but where no boundaries were in place, I did as I pleased. I wasn't lazy by nature, as at home I enjoyed helping mum out and making myself useful. I think it did simply boil down to my not being happy and finding my own way of dealing with that. I could have gone the other way by burying myself in school work but that didn't happen.

My lack of work for the "oranges" project may have caused Sister Julie to wash her hands of me but that in no way compared with what she came up against just a few weeks later. I wasn't the instigator of this little charade but I did take part, so all I can say is that I was very lucky not to have been caught or I would surely have been expelled.

One of the girls in the class had brought in a copy of Ian Fleming's *Dr No* which she had found lying around at home. We were having turns of borrowing the book overnight when it was accidentally left behind on one of the shared tables in the geography room. As nobody owned up to bringing the book into school, blame was apportioned equally to anybody who had taken part in the sinful act of reading the book. Sister Francis even put in a rare appearance to our classroom to question us and to warn us that if there was ever a repeat of such degraded behaviour then there would be serious consequences for whoever was responsible.

The class of '66 - with Miss Green

Miss Horner, who, it was generally understood was a retired English teacher from a bygone era, took us for elocution lessons. She really wasn't nice and seemed to derive pleasure from belittling us, often leaving the class at the end of the day with one of us in tears. She didn't leave me out but I didn't cry in school - I managed to hold it together until I went home. She took the weekly lesson in our form classroom for an hour at a time. Part of the lesson was spent standing with a book on our heads for deportment then for the rest of the time we had to recite a short verse which we were told to practice in front of a mirror, every day, to be tested on our pronunciation during the lesson. Some of the girls would practice but the rest of us picked up the wording as it went round the class. On the one occasion I was asked to recite the verse first, I developed a bad cough and had to miss my turn. Miss Horner did once tell me my speaking voice and pronunciation were perfect as my voice was coming through as clear as a bell, advising me to speak like that always. I had an absolutely streaming cold at the time.

She could be cruel at the best of times but she did something once to surpass all her other nastiness. She seemed to be on a particularly short fuse on the day which caused one of the girls who was quite shy and totally intimidated by Miss Horner, to be almost too scared to recite the verse. She did manage to speak, but very quietly with Miss Horner screaming at her to speak up. The more Miss Horner shouted, the more distressed the girl became, until Miss Horner yelled at her to get her mother to take her to the doctor to arrange surgery to have her mouth made bigger as it was too small for her to speak. You could have heard a pin drop in the room as we were all so shocked and disgusted. The lesson came to an end then later in the day, after lunch, Miss Horner burst into the room, interrupting the lesson. She was crying as she begged the girl to forgive her for what she had said. I don't know what prompted her to come back, whether she realised that she had gone too far or else the story had reached Sister Francis. I can only vaguely recall a story about the girl's dad visiting the school afterwards but am not sure what, if any action was taken. The following week didn't see any softening of Miss Horner's teaching methods.

Monica was always very well behaved at school,

settling down much better than I had. She worked well with good results. She tells me that Miss Horner would scream out if anybody ever dropped anything onto the floor. The class planned before one lesson, at precisely ten past the hour, to all drop a pencil on the floor. They did so but Miss Horner was so carried away on the crest of a wave of the Shakespeare she was reciting to her non captive audience that she didn't even notice.

Miss Concannon, the art teacher, went by the name of "Lady Conk" throughout the school, as she was so very refined and ladylike. We were never quite certain whether or not she was a real titled Lady but probably not as we addressed her as "Miss".

We had a separate teacher for craft lessons who joined the school when I was in the third year. She told us she had been at art college at the same time as John Lennon but that she didn't know him and had never actually met him. The fact that she may have breathed the same air as John Lennon was enough for us as we begged her for the tiniest scraps of information she could give us. She always laughed, repeating that she had absolutely nothing to say. We were never convinced and it was during our weekly, single geography lessons, again with Sister Julie, spent in our own classroom, that we found out that the craft teacher had a spare period and would be upstairs in the craft room. Some of us, myself included, took turns while Sister wrote on the blackboard to slip out of class and up the spiral staircase to the craft room to discuss John Lennon. If Sister Julie ever noticed we were missing then she never said.

School dinners were eaten in the huge dinner hall in the school basement, in two shifts. The food was cooked on the premises but wasn't very nice and didn't compare with the lovely food we had been served at St Mary's. Apart that is, from chips which we started having from the third year. We would know it was a chip day from when we first arrived at school at 9 o'clock in the mornings as the smell would fill the air at that time. Mornings spent with the prospect of chips for dinner went well. We were all very ladylike and at dinner times we sat at tables for either six or eight girls where the dinner ladies delivered the food to the tables in serving dishes. On our table each day when we were in the first and second years, we each added a contribution to either the gravy or the custard, which would be used by the older girls on the second sitting. We never put anything bad in, just such things as a pea would be added to the custard jug or currants to the gravy. The food might not have been that nice but I ate everything that was put in front of me. I could never understand how some of the other girls were "picky" eaters and would see genuine glances of concern from my friends sometimes as I ate what they turned their noses up at. I did, however, stop short of eating the school rice pudding which resembled a watery sludge. We would all groan so much when it was served that eventually, although it stayed on the menu, the teacher on dinner duty would announce that if anybody didn't want rice pudding they could leave the room, which would be followed by a mass exodus.

We had to spend the rest of dinner time in the school grounds as we were not allowed in the building apart from during wet weather and the only girls allowed out were those going home for dinner. I remember one incident when some of the girls were caught leaving the grounds to pop to a shop across the road. This was dealt with very severely and we were all threatened with expulsion if anybody was caught leaving the school grounds again. I understand that safety was paramount but there didn't seem to be any form of escalating scale for discipline in the school, it being either all or nothing.

Dancing lessons for the young ladies of Notre Dame

We were friendly with the school gardener, Dermot, and would often stop to chat with him as he worked in the grounds during our lunch hour, admiring his floral displays as the gardens, like the school building, were beautifully kept. On a spring afternoon in 1964 we stopped to look at a display which spelt out the name, "John". As Dermot walked towards us we were saying how we were surprised and impressed as we didn't know he was a Beatles fan. His face changed as he pointed out that the display had nothing to do with the Beatles, it was a tribute to John F Kennedy. We got the cold shoulder from Dermot for a while after that as we suspected he thought we were having a joke at his expense but we were serious.

My favourite teacher, and that of most of my classmates, had to be our form teacher, Miss Green, more commonly known as "Mouldy". There wasn't much love on either side at the start but she really did grow on us and by the time I left school, most of us were genuinely very fond of her. Besides teaching English, as our form teacher she had the responsibility for our religious lessons and the class in general. She would be aged around forty at the time and dressed differently to the other teachers, in clothes which were spectacularly old fashioned. On the first day back in the third year after the summer holidays, we sat at our desks waiting to see who was our form teacher for the year and when Mouldy walked in we all cheered while she grinned like a Cheshire cat. The same thing happened the following year but somebody had spotted her earlier, wearing a huge white dress decorated with multi coloured flowers, which we were told looked like curtain material. When she walked into our class most of us cheered but I couldn't as I had fallen off my chair laughing.

I sat my mock 'O' levels and didn't do too badly all things considered, although there would have been a lot of catching up to be done if I was to sit my

GCEs and I didn't want that. I had no idea what I wanted to do, apart from leave school. Mum made an appointment to see Sister Francis and returned home looking very relieved and quite excited. Sister Francis had told her about a new college which had just opened in Kirkby and if I really wanted to leave school then she suggested I enrol on the secretarial course offered by the college where I could learn shorthand and typing. I too was relieved, feeling like a weight had been lifted and I had been given another chance.

I had missed the entrance exam for the college but Sister Francis pulled some strings and I was able to take the exam, on my own, alone in the college hall. My test was marked and returned showing that I had the highest marks out of all the entrants for that year. I was very conscious of how I had let mum and dad down by not working at school and this result was another reason to kick myself. It did, however, boost my confidence, enough to wake me up to the fact that I could do well. I still can't explain fully why I never worked at Notre Dame.

I did well at college, passing everything with flying colours, including getting a grade A in English Language GCE 'O' level which was part of the course. I then felt as if I had gone some way to redeeming myself and making amends to mum and dad. Without the help of Sister Francis I don't know what I would have done after leaving school and have always been grateful to her.

I left college not as the new me but rather as the

more grown up version of the old me with my self esteem restored, having acquired the skills I needed to enter the great unknown of the working world.

Chapter Eight

The Workplace

During my first week after leaving college, mum accompanied me to the Labour Exchange in Leece Street where an interview was arranged for me with a small insurance company in Dale Street. I sat wide eyed throughout the interview with the manager and as this was to be my first job and I had nothing to compare it with, I agreed to start working the following Monday, as a junior shorthand typist. Mum and I then went to our favourite haunt at the railway cafe on Lime Street where I had my usual treat of a blackcurrant tart while mum had her usual cup of tea and a scone with jam and cream. The cafe was always busy with seating for over a hundred people and as was usually the case, we had to walk round looking for an empty table but when we were seated, we were waited on by ladies wearing black dresses with a white pinny and hat, who dashed around the huge room looking flustered, clattering the cups and saucers as they went. We would always try to find a window seat where we could watch the comings and goings at St George's Hall, which the cafe overlooked, and the rest of Liverpool go by.

That first job only lasted two weeks as, with mum and dad's permission, I gave a week's notice at the end of my first week. It was a strange place and not a bit like I had expected working life to be. My day to day duties were fine as I put my newly acquired skills into practice, but it was the staff I found decidedly strange. One of the girls went shoplifting at lunchtime then came back to show us what she had stolen, without any attempt at trying to keep it a secret. She came back after lunch one day with a tie for her dad's birthday, and when somebody said they hoped she had paid for it she said she had really wanted to pay and had been determined to, but as she had been kept waiting in the queue for so long and it was easy to walk out without paying, that's what she did. I still wonder how she ended up.

Following another trip to the Labour Exchange I had an interview at Liverpool Probation Office with the deputy Principal Probation Officer, who I remember thinking looked very old and stern and not the type of person I had ever spoken to before. The figures of authority in my life up until now had for the most part been the female teachers and I felt shy, sometimes intimidated and simply unused to mixing with men. Apart from dad that is, and my uncles, but my home environment was different of course. I was asked at the interview whether any of my family had a criminal record. I didn't have a problem with being asked as I presumed it to be a standard question, but when I confirmed that none of us had been in any trouble, he almost shouted, "What, you're one of eight children, living in Kirkby and nobody has been in trouble? That's amazing!" I felt insulted and very small. However, I did get the job and settled very well, working as a shorthand typist for the next few years. The working hours were 9.00 am to 5.30 pm Monday to Friday as well as three hours on a Saturday morning, for which I was paid the princely sum of £5 5s 0d per week, payable monthly in arrears. Saturday morning working was phased out for office workers generally over the next few years. It was here at the Probation Office that I met my good friend Sharon.

The office was situated on the third floor of an old building in Marybone, at the junction of Vauxhall Road and Hatton Garden, just off Dale Street in Liverpool city centre. The building was an unusual shape with windows set in a curved frontage, giving the appearance of jutting out onto the street. On arrival each morning we were met by Joe, an eighty year old man who operated a cage lift.

In some ways the Probation Office wasn't the best start for me as, much as the majority of the officers were very nice, they were figures of authority and in some ways like teachers. Even the older secretaries seemed to belong to the adult world which Sharon and I hadn't yet graduated to so we kept very much to ourselves. Not that I felt in any way unequal to the older girls, it was just that we didn't have much in common with them at a time when I thought of anyone over the age of twenty one as good as being middle aged. One of the girls in the office who was twenty four at the time started seeing a new boyfriend who she told us was about an inch shorter than her. I overheard her discussing him in the office, saying if they stayed together she would buy some flat heeled shoes. I can remember looking at her and thinking she was cutting it a bit fine to think she'd have so much as a boyfriend let alone a husband before too long.

I didn't have any problem talking to Joe in the lift on the way in and out of work which possibly had something to do with being at different ends of the age spectrum. Joe spent his days cooped up in the lift and took every opportunity to have a chat and gossip. I arrived for work one morning to be presented with a watch he had bought for me. I knew I couldn't accept it but had no idea what to say so I thanked him and took it home to show mum and dad. They told me how to handle the situation by explaining that I would just have to thank Joe but tell him the watch was too much to accept. Dad asked me questions and although I don't know exactly what he thought, he couldn't have suspected anything untoward from Joe or he would have been down to speak to him, and I am fairly sure he didn't do that. I didn't have too much of a problem returning the watch to Joe, because I realised he should have known better, but it was a bit embarrassing.

The office in Marybone has since been demolished and replaced with a new building having been erected on the same site. The ground floor is used as office space with very impressive looking student accommodation on the upper floors.

I smoked my first cigarette on the roof of that old building. My first attempt at smoking had been when I was twelve when Pauline and I hatched a plan to take not one to share, but two of my dad's untipped Players Navy Cut, to smoke at the hostel path. Neither of us were able to draw as much as a second puff on the cigarettes as we dropped them to the ground while we stood and retched.   A few years later at   Kirkby College we were allowed to smoke in the canteen and there would be a thick fog every lunch time from the sixteen and seventeen year olds puffing away, but I always refused to smoke for two reasons. Firstly, there was no way I could afford to buy cigarettes and secondly, while most people were saying yes to smoking, I liked to be a bit more individual by saying no.

Sharon smoked and used to nag me to have one with her at lunch times.   Eventually, one day I agreed, for peace sake really as I still had   no intention of being a smoker and so we climbed onto the office roof to smoke while we sunbathed. Sharon assumed we would repeat the process the following day, which we did as it seemed easier than arguing and besides, being up on the roof on our own, able to see for miles around, we could escape for an hour, as it didn't feel like we were on a grimy old roof in the centre of Liverpool.   After I had smoked five cigarettes in total with Sharon, she phoned in sick one day and as lunchtime approached, I decided to pop to the newsagents across the road to buy ten Players No. 6.   I went down to the toilet to light up and was promptly extremely sick, which may have been due to it being the first time I had smoked indoors and I was in an airless room, buried deep down inside the building. I threw the packet in the bin and that was the end of that - until the end of the day when I bought ten more on the way home because I felt the need. I did manage to quit, two and a half years ago, almost forty years later.

My work at the Probation Office was varied and I found it very interesting with no two days every really the same. For my first two years, as I was the youngest and most junior member of staff, it was my job to call at the head office just down the road in Crosshall Street on the way in each morning, to collect the daily court list. The list was to show the Probation Officers if any of their charges had been arrested the night before as if so, then they would have to accompany them to the Magistrates' Court, located on Dale Street, next to the old Main Bridewell. The Magistrates' Court was a dreary, bleak looking building, reached by walking through the high, black wrought iron gates surrounding the entrance which must have given a feeling of doom to whoever passed through to stand before the court.

After collecting the list each day, I had a short walk up Hatton Garden to our office, past the Fire Headquarters and in the vicinity of Higsons Brewery on Dale Street. The problem I had of feeling queasy in the mornings affected me more than at any other time as I walked up Hatton Garden on those mornings. The smell of the hops from the brewery filled the air, making me feel so sick that I would stand, watching people wandering happily up the road while I was trying very hard, in between taking deep breaths, not to be sick. Depending on which way the wind was blowing, some days were manageable but on other days I would have to take a detour and go the long way round, still balking as I made my way to work. I must have looked a sorry sight.   Whenever I asked people out of curiosity what they thought of the smell from the brewery, they either said they hadn't noticed or some even said they liked it.   By lunchtime I could walk down the road without any trace of sickness.

My first job of the day on arriving at the office was to make a huge pot of tea to set out with cups and saucers onto a table in the office kitchen used by the officers. As secretaries we remained at our desks to eat or drink as we were never invited to the kitchen, for which I was very grateful as I was so shy. After making the tea I would then go to my desk to press the nine extension buttons on a Bakelite telephone, to let the officers know their tea was made. They would then congregate in the kitchen for half an hour or so, to catch up with each other and to study the court list, after having taken bets on who might be on the list.

It was once suggested it might be a good idea for me to accompany the officer on daily juvenile court duty, to help look after the youngsters. I didn't agree but had to keep my thoughts to myself as one morning I found myself being left to mind a boy on my own, as the officer said he needed to speak to somebody, saying he would be back in a few minutes.   I stood side by side in a hallway outside the court room with the "juvenile delinquent", who disappeared within seconds of the officer leaving us, down Crosshall Street. A policeman went in hot pursuit of the boy to collar him and bring him back which brought an end to my short days of acting as chaperone, much to my relief.

My main duties in the office were answering the phone and greeting people through a hatch in the wall, as well as using my Pitman shorthand to take notes from the officers of weekly meetings with their probationers and their notes taken from home visits, court hearings and the typing up of Court reports.

I opened that hatch door one Saturday morning at 12 o'clock and slammed it shut again when I saw who was on the other side. It wasn't a dangerous criminal I was facing. As I gingerly opened the hatch again I had to explain to Julie who was now laughing, why I was wearing her red polo neck sweater. She had just finished work and had called with John to give me a lift home.

The day we received a notice advising we were due a "Time and Motion" inspection for the secretarial staff caused a degree of concern as there were times when we didn't really have much to do. This was due in part to some of the officers neglecting to dictate their notes, sometimes for weeks at a time, then when they did eventually get round to dictating they couldn't remember details of meetings if their notes were too scrappy. As this involved reporting on their many cases, it became a bit of a shambles as if their memories failed them then they made the notes up. Our boss, the Senior Probation Officer, had recently left and one of the other officers was acting senior. Out of concern at the prospect of reductions in staff, he hit upon the idea of us duplicating everything we had to type so by the time the inspectors called, we were fairly inundated with typing. This worked very well as we were all able to keep our jobs.

Reports for The Juvenile and Magistrates' Courts were typed on foolscap length forms printed on plain white paper with two carbon copies. Crown Court reports were a lot more difficult as they were typed on shorter, quarto sized, pale blue parchment paper, which turned out to be the most stressful document I have ever had to type on a regular basis.

Typing errors were erased by using either a pencil typewriter rubber or one in the shape of a wheel. Erasing on the blue paper inevitably wrecked the page as the paper would either disintegrate, leaving a hole or at best a white mark where the colour had been removed. We had to make six carbon copies to be passed around the Crown Court. The officers marked themselves in and out of the office on a blackboard in the general office and Mr Joseph, who was the resident officer on Crown Court duty, would sign out every morning at ten to ten, calling, "Crown" on his way out. I would hold my breath when he returned after the court closed if he had taken one of my reports because the judges were always complaining at the poor quality and how the bottom copies were illegible. If your typewriter roller had worked loose, then the paper wouldn't grip and the bottom copies would slide, with words disappearing and falling towards the edge of the paper. I would sit banging away at the keys, trying to make a good imprint through to the bottom copy but as I was so nervous my fingers would often land on the wrong key. The Crown Court reports were usually less detailed than the others and a lot shorter so I would occasionally type them out twice to give good copies, while hoping the judge wouldn't notice and complain that the copies didn't match.

Typewriters were serviced under contract periodically when the rollers would be oiled and the keys cleaned. I never found two typewriters the same to work on, either manual or electric. Some of the keys on the old manual machines never loosened up and you had to hammer away at them, slowing you down, while you could fly away on others as fast as your fingers and brain would allow. At other times one or two of the keys would stick, causing a pile up and a black splodge in the middle of your neatly typed page. After walking in to work on a freezing cold winter morning you could barely move your fingers across the keys until they had thawed out and it could take up until about 10 o'clock and a hot drink before you stopped shivering and were able to type properly. Having a machine with loose keys made such a difference as to how fast you could get through your work as with a machine in good working order, regardless of its age, you could type at a speed of anything up to about 80 wpm which was quite impressive considering all that was involved in producing a document of quality.

Typing on a manual typewriter involved using the carriage return bar, while keeping your ears open for the little warning bell as you were getting close to the right margin, as well as watching that you didn't run off the bottom edge of the page. All too many times it happened that you thought you could squeeze one more line onto a page to avoid leaving too big a gap at the bottom, only to see the paper slip in the roller causing the words to disappear which meant ripping the page up and starting again.

Operating the typewriter involved manually setting up a document to prepare for typing, such as setting tabs for columns or centering a heading before you started to type. You had to first count the number of spaces available between the side margins, count the number of characters in your heading, subtract one from the other, halve the difference and indent that amount of spaces before typing the heading. To underline your heading you would go back to the start of the line and press the underline key under each character or if you wanted to underline in red, then you could press another key to release the red half of your typewriter ribbon. To set tabs for columns you divided the number of columns by the amount of spaces between the left and right margins then once the tabs were set, you didn't need to look at the keyboard or the paper in the machine as you could fly away, tabbing between each column.

Typewriter ribbons lasted for months, working round spools on either side of the machine, to be discarded when the typing became too faint. I always left mine until the words were barely legible, to avoid having to "run in" a new ribbon to get rid of surplus ink which would clog up your keys and besides, faint typing was easier to rub out. After typing with a new ribbon I would then sit with a paper clip clearing the letters which didn't print clearly.

There was a a bit of a commotion one morning as I walked into Crosshall Street to collect the court list. The Principal Probation Officer for Liverpool was based at that office and there was a huddle of people surrounding his secretary. I peered over somebody's shoulder wondering what all the excitement was about, to see that she had an electric typewriter. She was saying how she didn't like it, having been so used to her trusty old one but she did eventually get to like it and within a couple of years I had one myself.

Probation Orders were given for offences of petty theft, or larceny as it was known at the time, as well as for other fairly minor offences. We also had a sprinkling of working girls on probation for soliciting. Probation reports would be prepared whenever a child or youth was arrested, sometimes resulting in custodial sentences for the more serious crimes, or for regular offenders, who could be sent to approved schools, detention centres, borstal or prison, sometimes in steady progression. The officer would then correspond or visit the person in custody for the duration of their stay.

The Probation Service also offered a free service in marriage guidance, where anybody experiencing matrimonial problems could see an officer voluntarily. Some of the officers were unmarried and single but presumably they had some sort of training to qualify to advise. I was eighteen before I was allowed to take notes of the matrimonial cases but would sometimes overhear the officers discussing cases which they seemed to find amusing.

Amongst the regulars who passed through the office doors were a family by the name of Kenny, made up of up about ten children, siblings and cousins, with one or more of their names always appearing on our lists.

Two years ago while I was delving into genealogy, I had been searching for the maiden name of my maternal great grandmother. I had found records showing that she had been widowed and remarried so I had her first married name but couldn't find her birth name in any of the BDM records. Eventually, after searching the parish records of Liverpool Catholic churches I found an entry of her first marriage at St Anthony's church on Scotland Road. I read that she had been born in Co Meath in Southern Ireland, as Jane Kenny.

The 1901 census showed that the family had settled at No 4 Lower Milk Street, just a stone's throw away from our office in Marybone. From the census, it appeared that a family of brothers occupied four of the houses in the road as the residents all bore the same surname of Kenny. I had to smile to myself when I saw the name and details of the address, wondering if each time I opened the hatch at the probation office to speak to one of the Kenny boys, I had been facing a distant cousin.

I entered my newly found great grandmother's name onto a genealogy website, which as I have said, was two years ago now. Jane Kenny was the last name I entered on the site and I had forgotten having done so until yesterday when it was brought back to my attention in a very unexpected and surprising way. I switched my computer off at about half past eleven last night after I had finished noting the above about my search of the church records. The events were going round in my head still, as I hadn't switched my thoughts off. Just before I went to bed I had a last look at my mobile phone, as I usually do last thing at night, to see if any texts or emails had come through. I had one new email which literally made me jump when I read it. It was from a genealogy site and read:-

"Was Jane Kenny married at the time of the 1901 census?

We have found clues to Jane Kenny's married name, Doyle in the 1901 census.........."

Two of the women officers I worked with who were both in their early thirties, had left nursing careers to train as Probation Officers. They both said they thought I would make a good nurse and encouraged me to apply to train. I was swept along and was eventually persuaded to apply to Walton Hospital. Dad sat me down and tried to talk me out of it, pointing out how nurses were poorly paid and I would be giving up a good job with prospects, but I went ahead anyway even though I knew he was right, not liking to admit that I had changed my mind or indeed that it was never what I wanted in the first place.

The entry requirements for a student nurse at that

time were either five GCE 'O' levels or to sit an entrance exam. I sat the exam, again on my own, as I had just missed out on the student intake for that year. I sat in a large room, with just me and a male invigilator and can remember being embarrassed that my stomach was rumbling all the way through the exam. The man smiled at me as he took my paper, saying I could go to the canteen for some lunch while it was marked. He asked me to return to wait outside the exam room which I did until he returned, again smiling as he asked me to follow him to the Matron's office. After sitting wondering what happens next, I was ushered into a cosy little room with armchairs where I met the Matron who sat facing me at her desk, with a pot of tea. When I was relating the tale to dad later he said I should have been offered a cup of tea as it was rude of the matron not to do so. As she would most likely have a steady succession of visitors throughout the day, I said I thought it would be acceptable for her to forgo the niceties in a busy hospital. The matron chatted to me before handing me my marked paper, telling me how I would do well, as academics make good nurses. It's words like those few from the Matron that I've tried to remember through the years whenever my confidence has faltered and I have always been grateful to the Matron for saying it.

My "nursing day" has become something of a joke over the years and Monica will sometimes ask me if I still have the nurses' dictionary she bought for me. I refer to it as such as that's how long it lasted - one day. As a student nurse I had to live in the nurses hall and I stayed the one night before starting in a classroom the following morning. The classroom was possibly the final straw to make me realise the mistake I had made. I went home to see everyone at the end of the day on the No. 92 bus, in my green nurses dress, where the bus conductor quietly refused to take my fare as he gave me a nod of respect. When I reached home I went straight upstairs to sit on my bed and cried my eyes out. Margaret told mum and dad how upset I was and after talking to them, they said I didn't have to go back. Dad wrote a note for the Matron and drove down to the hospital to hand in the note, along with the keys to my room.

As I was now without a job, dad, with my best interests at heart, suggested I joined the Civil Service where I would have good prospects. He told me how well Auntie Maureen had done and how she would retire with a good pension. At seventeen, a pension was as good a prospect to me as dying and much as I was very fond of Auntie Maureen, I didn't want to be like her. However, I passed an entrance exam for the Civil Service but what I really wanted was to return to the Probation Office. I went along to see my old boss who took me back, as my job hadn't yet been filled. He did ask me was it not just the thought of the change that had brought me back, which was probably not far from the truth.

I first came across the mod cons of the office world such as Tippex correction strips, then later, its liquid form, after I had moved on from the Probation Service. Tippex was one of the first stepping stones from the Dickensian world into the ease of the modern office, followed by such delights as the photocopier which came into general use during the late 1960s. Prior to this anything to be duplicated for distribution round the office would be typed out on a Gestetner or Banda machine, the very name of which could conjure up an instrument of torture to me. My experience of using the Gestetner was not good, producing the messiest, most unprofessional looking copies ever. Operated by firstly rolling a long sheet known as a "skin", through your typewriter, you then typed onto the skin by hammering the keys down to make sure they cut through. The imprint of the lettering would be barely visible on the surface as the skin just looked as if it was covered in pin holes by the time you had finished, making it difficult to read through to check what you had typed. Having deciphered as best you could, any mistypes were corrected by painting on a thick, red liquid, a bit like nail varnish, then waiting for it to dry, which took forever, before typing over the spot again. I never knew the correction fluid to dry out completely so it was always touch and go as to how the page would turn out. The skin was then rolled round a drum, collecting ink randomly as it went, resulting in the printed sheet.

Working in an accountants office in London in the early 1970s, I had the pleasure of using the elite of typewriters, namely the IBM Golfball, with proportional spacing. Each letter took up a different amount of spaces, for instance the letter "i", would use one space whereas the "m" would take four and the capital "M" five spaces. To correct typing errors you had to backspace the right amount of times to remove the error. The letters were set on a small ball which gave the typewriter its name. The ball hit the page when the corresponding key was pressed. Not only was this the best typewriter ever, as it was, it also had a correction tape, which meant the day had arrived when I could say goodbye to a typewriter rubber - for that particular machine at least.

The final step up to the word processing package on a computer was an electronic typewriter with a memory whereby you could type, then sit and watch as the keys whizzed along by themselves, as if by magic.

When first told about word processors, they sounded to me like something from the space age. I was fascinated by the idea of lining up the text at the right margin as well as on the left side. While working for a most eccentric solicitor at one point, long before the advent of word processors, he had called me into his office to ask could I not line my typing up on the right side of the page as I had done on the left, on my typewriter. He shouted when I told him I didn't think it was possible, telling me to shut the door on my way out. I couldn't do that either but didn't intend to hang around to remind him that his office door was free standing, leaning against his office wall as he had removed it by the hinges some weeks earlier, for reasons best known to himself.

I enrolled on a short course to learn the basics of word processing and then six months later, at which time I was working as a "temp", to fit in with school times for my children, I had an assignment at a solicitors' office. When I arrived at the office my heart sank as I was ushered to a desk with one of the newfangled Amstrad computers sitting on it. It wouldn't have been so bad if the agency had told me, giving me a chance to brush up on my notes or to bring them with me. While I was musing about this, my attention was caught by one of the secretaries who was being consoled by her colleagues. I heard her saying that she had hardly slept the night before and didn't know what she was going to do, etc. I thought she must have a real family problem. Then from what I could hear, I realised that her problem was the new computer sitting on her desk. It turned out that the staff had all had tuition on how to use the word processors but none of them were happy about it and this particular woman was on the edge of breaking down altogether.

I asked if somebody could just refresh my memory because, like them, I hadn't actually used the machine but they all backed away in horror, apologising as they said they couldn't help. Realising I had to either figure out how to use the machine or go home, I managed to switch on, open a document, type a letter and save it. Then I noticed an error on the screen and couldn't remember how to get back in to alter it. After sitting there, dredging my brain long enough to make me start panicking, I was just about to admit defeat when I remembered the "edit" key and I was on my way, never to look back.

One difference I noticed when I was first able to correct errors by editing a screen was something I've never heard anybody else mention, and that is, whenever I had hit the wrong key on a typewriter, either manual or electric, I would know I had made a mistake. However, from when I first used a word processor, even though I would be conscious sometimes of hitting the wrong key, somehow I had lost that sense of knowing instinctively that I had made a mistake and it's only when I proof read that I see the errors.

The misconception that you don't need to be able to spell when using a word processor is something I have heard said many times. The red underline certainly helps by highlighting misspelt words, or the use of the spell checker will show obvious errors but this doesn't guarantee all mistakes are covered. As an example, while working at a particularly busy and understaffed solicitors' office, we were joined by a new member of staff, Lesley, who had impressed the practice manager by having just completed a legal secretarial course at college, whilst the rest of us had merely picked it up as we went along, over the years. Lesley couldn't spell to save her life, and neither could she type as it happened, but it was the spelling that caused a problem for the rest of us. She would constantly interrupt us to ask how to spell the most simple of words until one day when she asked me how to spell the word "saw" as in "I saw a bus", I suggested she looked in the big dictionary she spent more time reading than doing anything else. She replied, "I have done and it says its a cutting tool."

Just before spending a couple of years working in London when I was first married, I worked for a few months for one of the local building firms in Kirkby, whose office was situated on the industrial estate.

It was a family firm, run by three brothers, with an office staff of around twenty people. When I say that the brothers were contracted to build the ill fated artificial ski slope, on the East Lancashire Road, then anybody who has ever lived in Kirkby is likely to smile, as the ski slope that never was, or not for long anyway, is still talked about today.

One reported version of the events surrounding the ski slope as to why it was built in the first place, was that when Kirkby Urban District Council was due to merge with Knowsley Council, any funds remaining at Kirkby would be swallowed up by Knowsley. In an attempt to keep the money in Kirkby, one of the councillors came up with the idea of the ski slope as a sports facility for Kirkby, which could be built within the time constrains remaining for Kirkby Council.

Stories abounded at the time of how the slope wasn't a solid mound of earth, and had not been built in accordance with the plans, but instead was built on builders' rubble as the site was alleged to have been advertised locally as a dumping ground. There were also stories of children being used as cheap labour to lay the top layer of the slope.

Other reports were that planning permission had not

been granted as Kirkby didn't own the land, which in fact belonged to Liverpool Corporation. It was also said that the project had not been sanctioned by the Council. Then the final condemnation for the slope was when it was said to have been built facing the wrong way, onto the East Lancashire Road and as it was then deemed to be unsafe, it was demolished.

From what I remember of the brothers, the eldest one always turned up for work immaculately dressed in a business suit, shirt, tie and polished shoes, and quite often would head into the city centre at the end of the day to wine and dine. I didn't have much to do with him as he seemed to be constantly in discussions either on the phone or in person. and besides, I was just a bit wary of him as he wasn't the sort of boss I was accustomed to. The middle brother who was always affable, would turn up two or three times a week on his bike, with a story to tell after his wife had confiscated his car keys after a night on the tiles; while the third and youngest brother was the most down to earth and the most astute of the three, being the one who always knew exactly what was going on and where everybody was up to.

As the building of the ski slope progressed, slowly, as it seemed to be plagued by hold ups, whenever I asked the youngest brother just when it would be finished as it seemed to be going on for a long time, he would say there had been a slight hitch but all would be well, the slope would be finished and I was promised the first ride when it opened.

The Councillors often attended meetings at the office which would go on until after we had finished work for the day. I shared an office with the firm's accountant, while the rest of the office staff occupied a separate building across the yard, apart from one lady who worked just mornings with me. We were never overworked and I would often have time on my hands so one afternoon when I was invited to join a meeting in the brothers' office, I did so happily, watching the look of disapproval from the accountant as I closed the door behind me.

I was handed a drink in a tea cup, poured from a lemonade bottle, and told to be careful as it was very potent. It was around half past three in the afternoon when I started to sip the drink slowly, as instructed. In fact I'm not sure if I ever finished it. What I do remember is the men talking and me needing to spend a penny and trying to stand up without falling over, all within the space of about half an hour. I was in a room with eight men, five of whom were from the Council. They were talking shop and didn't seem to notice as I did manage to stand up to exit the room to cross the yard to the ladies room. By the time I came out of the toilet after being quite sick, the rest of the staff had gone home, having locked the door behind them, leaving me inside as they thought I'd gone home.

I made my way to the switchboard to phone home but it was one of those old fashioned types where you had to plug a cord in to get a line and I ended up with the lines like spaghetti, without managing to make a call. Another hour passed during which time

I had sobered up considerably and luckily for me the doors were unlocked as the cleaners arrived.

I never did have the first go on the ski slope as I had long since moved away by the time it was finished. The story didn't end with its demolition though, as prison sentences were ordered for some of those involved.

We've all heard it said how in the good old days you could walk out of a job on a Friday and into a new one on the Monday, which was quite true.

Column 42 in the Liverpool Echo classified section advertised the Situations Vacant for office workers. We didn't need CVs in those days. Most employers would print their phone number in the Echo for you to simply ring to arrange an interview when you would impart the details of your skills and employment history. You could be asked to take a shorthand and typing test which would last no more than a few minutes. Having established you qualified for the job you were then hired. It was so simple. For the more senior jobs the process could be a bit more involved, such as when I went to work at Liverpool University where I was interviewed by a panel of three people, but even then the interview was arranged over the phone.

I have never belonged to a Union and have never known an office worker who did. I have heard of the Shop and Office Workers Union but as I say, I never knew of any members. Consequently, office workers didn't have any rights and could be sacked instantly without any reason having to be given. This was good in some instances where the sacking was justified but it wasn't always fair. The saying used to be that if the boss didn't like your face it was enough to sack you and I did see a girl sacked once on her third day because the boss didn't like her make up.

The use of plain English in the workplace seems to be fast disappearing, to be replaced by jargon, which in turn seems to be increasing at a rate of knots, making it hard to keep up. I have no idea where the jargon comes from, or whether there is a think tank dedicated to the subject. One of the first new era jargon words I remember was "criteria" which came into use in the present century, although not always in the right context. Since then we have had a steady stream of new expressions coming into use it would seem, by the day. I prefer to stick to the old way of talking but we have to move with the times, although there is one turn of phrase that really gets under my skin. I just wonder what was wrong with saying "you" and "me" which have been replaced with "yourself" and "myself", especially during telephone conversations. It sounds so insincere and puts me in mind of somebody bowing and scraping, ready to kiss your feet. A telephone conversation could go along the lines of, "Yourself spoke to myself last week........."

Recently, I observed a "Team Leader", conducting a "One to One", with a customer services person with the title of "Liaison Officer", in a call centre. I jotted down some of the words used by the Team

Leader during the fifteen minute session, as follows:-

Focus, the next level, going forward, skill set, high energy, upskill, upsell, gatekeeper, positive, team (repeatedly), heads up, it's all about, spreadsheet. It seemed from what I heard that the solution to many a problem could be found by sticking it on a spreadsheet.

As this was on a hot, summer's day, a member of staff made a passing comment that they would like an ice cream. Before the words were barely out of his mouth, an email went round the "team" from the deputy team leader with the title of "Lead Rep", with the words, "Team Ice Cream" in the subject line, asking who would like to partake of a team ice cream. She was serious.

Other popular words and practices in the office environment are "admin", which seems to be the word used for anything to do with a piece of paper, telephone, keyboard, or any form of office communication; "desk change" which involves moving people from where they sit in their open plan office, to sit beside somebody they don't particularly like; "Are you having a nice day so far?", which started out with the the American, "Have a nice day" which everybody seemed to think funny before we adopted it ourselves; "bond", (whether you like a person or not); "number crunching"; "can do attitude"; "hit the ground running" and "no brainer". I'm sure we didn't use jargon during my early working days, I certainly don't remember any. Everything was just "gear", apart, that is from the gobbledegook used in professions such as in legal offices.

Thinking back over the past ten to twenty years or so, there is one word which has been bandied about a lot which I still hear today although not as often now. It's the word often used to describe the type of candidate an employer is seeking. The word is, "bubbly". Margaret once read out a job advert to me from the Liverpool Echo, asking for a "bubbly" person. She then asked, "Does that mean they are looking for somebody full of wind?"

Job titles have also changed, where a shop assistant can now be a "colleague" while supervisors are the "team leaders". A quick glance at a job website will show that a dinner lady is now a "Lunchtime Welfare Assistant" which could presumably include dinner men, as I don't recall reading of any equal opportunity exclusions for the post. A salesman/woman is an "Outbound Sales Generator" who may sometimes have to "Up-sell" which I gather has something to do with selling over and above what the customer wants; and a cleaner is a "Cleaning operative". I saw an advert some time ago for a "Chilled colleague" which I assumed was for work at the fresh food or freezer section in a supermarket. Whether or not somebody had their wires crossed I'm not sure but I went on to read that the position was to "meet and greet" at the store.

Before I leave the office environment, where I have seen so many changes and advancements through the years, I would just like to give a mention to my favourite addition, apart of course from the computers, and that is the Post-it note.

Chapter Nine

Entertainment and Technology

I remember the day vividly, shortly after my fourth birthday, that I sat facing the corner where our first television set was being installed. I watched fascinated, waiting for the men to finish. I don't remember how I came to believe they were going to put "the little people" inside the set but I do remember dad saying they would be put in last, just before the back went on. I also remember turning to look at the door, wondering when the men were coming back because they hadn't put the people in yet, before it dawned on me that I'd been had.

The wireless had always been around to listen to of course, although I took that for granted and don't have any recollection of questioning where the voices came from.

That could well have been my first experience of feeling embarrassed and I have sometimes wondered since if it was normal for a four year old to believe that was how a television worked. Thinking about it now, at that age it was natural to believe amazing things did happen, such as how my little sister had recently appeared miraculously overnight, having been sent down from heaven. I had no reason to doubt dad's word when I asked him how I could dream about fairies and he told me all I had to do was go to sleep while thinking about them, reassuring me that that was how he managed to dream about fairies every night. I hadn't yet quite grasped the difference between the real and the unreal as I still believed anything could happen if you wanted it enough and while I waited, I could pretend. I was soon to learn that the pretending never stops, when I saw that grown ups had switched from reading the fairy tales to reading or viewing fictitious tales of romance, thrillers or science fiction, simulating real life events or making up unreal ones. What I understood to be my imagination, the grown ups called entertainment, both of which amounted to the same thing - taking time out from reality.

We rented that first television set. Other options available were to either buy a set outright, buy on hire purchase or to use the "pay as you view" facility by inserting a sixpenny piece into a slot attached to the set to top up the meter, this method being introduced a bit later on. Luckily, we always rented our set on a monthly basis, with uninterrupted viewing.

The very first television programmes I watched on BBC were "*Listen with Mother*" for pre school children which included *Picture Book*, *Andy Pandy*, *Bill and Ben*, *Rag, Tag and Bobtail* and the *Woodentops* and when there was nothing else on during the day, the Test Card would be displayed with music playing which I liked to study sometimes to see if the picture changed. As older children we looked forward to "*Children's Hour*" when we came home from school, to watch such memorable programmes as *Crackerjack* hosted by Leslie Crowther.

With the BBC providing our first viewings and ITV first broadcasting in 1955, entertainment was provided to suit all tastes, apart, that is, from those who didn't approve of television, per se, like Pauline's dad, who refused to have a set in the house. When ITV first introduced us to *Z Cars* in 1962 we had some, perhaps misplaced pride in the fact that, set in the fictitious town of Newtown, the programme was said to have been based on Kirkby, although it remained a mystery as to where it was actually filmed. There were occasional sightings reported in the area of a blue Ford Anglia as used by the police in the programme, flitting past, but that could well have been our dad as he had the same model at the time. Broadcast on Wednesdays at 7.00 pm, the programme coincided with the evening Pauline and her family went, every week, religiously, into Walton to visit her auntie and family. Pauline told me at some point that they went deliberately on Wednesdays so her dad could watch *Z Cars*.

Being very different to Mr Bolton who had dismissed television out of hand, refusing to have one in the house, our dad welcomed it. That didn't stop his censorship as he decided what we could and couldn't watch and if he deemed something as unsuitable, then he would ban it.

All ten of us crowded into the back room one evening in 1962, ready to watch "ourselves" on the television, having heard the rumours that a programme featuring characters based on real life people from "up north" was about to start. We'd heard that some people believed Coronation Street was to be a documentary, actually showing the lives of real people, and we all laughed at the prospect of our family going public or at who would possibly agree to being shown "live" on television. We then settled down to watch and all went well, as we took in the various characters and tried to pick up the "plot" if indeed there was one, until the Rovers Return scene came into view. Dad didn't like it, and he drowned out the sound from the crackly old set in the corner, as he ranted about how they were encouraging people to spend their time and their wages in the "bloody pub". That saw the end of our viewing permission as dad banished the programme, telling us that if he caught any of us watching it again, he would cut the plug off. Of course he never did cut the plug on the many occasions he caught us watching Coronation Street because he liked television as much as the rest of us. He would just walk in, say, "Turn that bloody rubbish off" and turn to the BBC.

I still watch "Corrie" and admit that I can't imagine how I would feel if I ever saw it come to an end. I've read that over 5000 characters have come and mostly gone throughout the life of the programme but once they're gone, they're gone as far as I'm concerned as we don't dwell on the past in soaps - we need the stimulation of exciting plots happening now or on the horizon. It isn't the characters that keep us viewing; the story lines range from being as mundane as our everyday lives, interspersed with the occasional gripping disaster, murder etc. when we can't wait for the next thrilling instalment, so it isn't particularly the content, as I could live without those bursts of excitement. I'm pretty sure I would survive the demise of Coronation Street but I know I would miss it as it has remained a constant, through the good and not so good times, since my childhood, and it would leave an empty space if it ended.

It wasn't just dad who censored our viewing. Mum was the "bad language" monitor. It must have been hard for her to relax while watching television with the rest of us at times, as the second a swear word was so much as hinted at then she would be out of her chair like lightening to switch off. Even worse than bad language was anything with remotely immoral connotations. We once heard the word "pregnant" used in a programme and mum couldn't get out of her chair quick enough to switch off although there were times as she was reaching for the off button that you'd see the tears start in her eyes as she was trying not to laugh.

I often think back to mum and dad's reactions and wonder what dad especially, would make of today's television. While listening to local radio recently I heard a very well respected radio presenter describe some television as "toxic". I couldn't have put it better myself and as for dad, I very much suspect that we may have seen at least one set disappearing through a window if he was here today.

Amongst my other personal favourite programmes of the 60s were *The Adventures of Robin Hood*, watched on Saturday afternoons; *Armchair Theatre* on Sunday nights; *The Black and White Minstrel Show* which was one of mum's favourites, *Hancock's Half Hour* - one of dad's favourites; *The Liver Birds*; *Opportunity Knocks*; *Please Sir*, *Randall and Hopkirk (deceased)*; *The Sky at Night* and *Dr Finlay's* Casebook, to name just a few.

I can't really comment on sports programmes because I have never watched any, apart from cup finals or other big football matches. Even though Saturday afternoons were generally given over to sport at home, with *Match of the Day*, I would try to make sure I was out, not only because I didn't want to watch sport but because you couldn't breathe if Gerry was at home watching an Everton away match to win, or a Liverpool match, to lose. He would sit, telling anybody who breathed too loudly to hush, and God help mum if she ever thought she could get the hoover out, as he sat glued to the television with the radio blurring away beside him, in case he missed anything. The thing was, mum would ignore him and would carry on as usual, with the hoover, singing at the same time, so it was best to be out of the house. There would be a distinct air of despondency if Everton lost but high spirits and the joys of spring if they won and on those occasions, if I happened to be around when Gerry came home later after celebrating "their" win, then he would pay me well to make him a fried egg butty.

I arrived home from work one Friday evening, the night before a Liverpool - Everton derby match, to find Gerry walking round swinging a hammer. When he brought it over and put it down on the tea table and I realised he wasn't actually using the hammer to knock any nails in, I asked him what it was for and he said, "This is what Liverpool are going to get tomorrow." Gerry and Eddie and their respective sons are still loyal to Everton.

In a class of their own were the Westerns which we all loved to watch, despite the fact that they were about cowboys, which seemed incidental to the plot as we followed the lives of characters such as the Cartwright family in *Bonanza;* Clint Eastwood in *Rawhide*; the adventures of Clint Walker as *Cheyenne*; *The Lone Ranger* - the good deed cowboy who we followed week by week hoping to catch a glimpse of his face without the eye mask he always wore, which we never did; and *Wagon Train*. Then of course there were the John Wayne type cowboy and Indian films, shown on Sunday afternoons, which didn't have the continuity interest of the serials, although I could be persuaded to sit through the occasional one of those, as well as watching Westerns at the pictures. In fact, Lee Marvin's *Paint Your Wagon* is amongst one of my all time favourite films of that era, next to Audrey Hepburn in *My Fair Lady* and *Fiddler on the Roof.*

We howled laughing when we were little at such programmes as *Billy Bunter, Old Mother Riley, Popeye* and *The Flintstones*. Later on we progressed to watching the antics of Frankie Howerd and the "Carry On" films, although I would find it hard to bring myself to watch these now even though I see they are still shown. The funniest television I have ever watched is Harry Secombe, Spike Milligan and Peter Sellers in *The Telegoons* with *Monty Python's Flying*

211

Circus which began at the end of the 1960s, coming a close second. So much comedy is dated and although some of *Monty Python* over the years could still make me smile, I wonder if I would find *The Telegoons* funny now, as from what I remember it bordered on the hysterical. One series, however, which has never stopped making me laugh, even today, no matter how many times I have watched it, which began in the 1970s, is *Fawlty Towers*.

The Beverly Hillbillies was a classic comedy shown each weekday at 6.00 pm. during the 60s. Most of the people I knew watched it as it was quite hilarious and something which was never to be forgotten once seen.

We enjoyed horror films throughout the 1960s such as Alfred Hitchcock's classic and legendary *Psycho* as well as *The Birds*. Julie came home after watching *Psycho* when it was first released and I listened as she told me all about it, including the shower scene, only to be disappointed when she told me I was too young to see it myself. I did get to see it when it was re-released several years later when I was just about old enough to get into the pictures to be frightened first hand.

Performances by Boris Karloff, Christopher Lee and Peter Cushing were unique as they portrayed Dracula and Frankenstein without any of the wonders of today's cinematography. All it took to start me twitching and looking over my shoulder, knowing I'd spend the night with the light on, was the sight of lightening over a Transylvanian castle, or a look in the eyes of Boris Karloff, with or without the bolt through his neck.

My single, most memorable episode of any television programme ever, was watched one evening at Auntie Margaret and Uncle Tom's pub in West Kirby, over the water, on the Wirral. It has been reported that 25 million people watched the final episode to see justice done as Dr Richard Kimble, played by David Janssen, shook hands with Sgt Gerrard, in *The Fugitive*. After watching Dr Kimble for four years as he was chased by Sgt Gerrard after being falsely accused of murdering his wife, we saw him finally find the person he in turn had chased, the real murderer, the one armed man.

The pop programmes of the day were *Juke Box Jury*, which aired from 1959 to 1967, hosted by David Jacobs with a celebrity panel to judge new releases and cast their vote as to whether they thought the record would be a hit or a miss. *Ready Steady Go* was another favourite pop show of the era, but it was *Top of the Pops* that was to become the staple of my teenage years as far as television was concerned and the one programme never to be missed. Shown at 7 o'clock every Thursday, we would have spent the day speculating on the record that would be at number one in the charts. The songs from the top twenty were played from new arrivals into the charts, as well as those moving up towards the top, ending with the No. 1. From 1968 Flick Colby choreographed Pans People who danced to one record each week when an artiste wasn't able to attend in person.

During those early days of television, the programmes finished at the end of the day firstly by playing the National Anthem on the BBC, followed by a high pitched beeping sound, in case anybody had forgotten to switch off or had fallen asleep in their armchair. A white dot would then appear in the centre of the screen before everything went black, until the morning. Eddie once said he fell asleep in the chair one night and was woken by a voice from the television saying, "Haven't you forgotten something?" I think he was joking or dreaming maybe.

The first mention I heard of "videos" was while visiting a friend. She was telling a group of us how we would soon be able to hire films from shops for £1.00 a time, to watch in our own homes, where we could perhaps have friends and family round, just like at the pictures. I listened, enthralled, thinking it sounded liked something from America. Before long, we were told, no home would be without a video player which meant that apart from watching films, it would no longer matter if a television programme was missed because it could be recorded.

Most of us today will at least have heard of an "app" in relation to technology, even if it's something we have seen on the adverts without knowing or being interested in what it is. We had one "app" as teenagers, short for "appendage", which came in the form of a transistor radio, or trannie. The trannie was our essential link to the world of music and something we couldn't exist without.

I listened to Radio Luxembourg when it came on air from 7.00 o'clock in the evenings, but during the daytime, it was the pirate radio station, Radio Caroline, broadcasting from the waters just off Ramsey in the Isle of Man, that was my life's blood. I don't say that lightly because music mattered, so much.

Our teenage years were spent basking in the glory of Liverpool, which, along with my school friends, I believed was the best place in the world to be. We had two of the best football teams in Britain; Liverpool had already produced countless stars such as Ken Dodd, Frankie Vaughan, Rex Harrison, Arthur Askey, Kenny Everett, George Melly and Rita Tushingham and then the Mersey Sound emerged, churning out such talent as Cilla Black, The Swinging Blue Jeans, Gerry and the Pacemakers, Billy J Kramer, Billy Fury, The Searchers and, of course, The Beatles.

As teenagers we belonged to one of two tribes at the time - the Mods or the Rockers and whenever we met up out of school on trips into town or to Formby woods, meeting other such groups on the buses or trains, we would call out to each other asking if we were a Mod or a Rocker. I didn't quite know what I was when I was asked. I knew what I aspired to be but somehow, dressed in a cotton dress and summer sandals I felt I didn't look the part of either really, but decided that I looked more like a Mod so that's what I claimed to be. What I never told anybody at the time was that I didn't actually like some of the Beatles music. I preferred the Rolling Stones.

I heard it said around the time of "Beatlemania" that every Scouser had a link to the Beatles and our family was no exception. While I was beavering away at Kirkby College on my secretarial course, along with some of my fellow students, I spent a wet Saturday afternoon walking round Kirkby town centre carrying a collection box for charity. When I arrived home, one of Julie's friends was sitting in the front room with her boyfriend who was George Harrison's elder brother. I stood looking at him with my mouth open as we were introduced, wondering if I was imagining it, and thinking how my college friends would never believe me. That turned out to be quite true as when I ran into college on the following Monday morning, bursting with my news, hardly anybody blinked an eye, either that or they weren't so easily impressed.

When the Beatles played at the Cavern at lunch times, which was before my time, Julie went once or twice during the early days, when it was just a dingy cellar. Dad, never short of an opinion, would roar with laughter at his own jokes, saying how that's where they should have stayed and he wouldn't go to see them if they were playing in the back garden. He was equally non-magnanimous about Cilla, saying she sounded like one of the women at Paddy's Market calling out, "Dem oranges, a penny each".

We will all have our favourites from amongst the

outstanding performers who have earned our admiration and respect over the years. They have gone by differing names through the years, such as music hall entertainer, silent movie star, performer, singer, dancer, actor/actress, acrobat, magician, comedian, etc. The list isn't exhaustive but more recently a collective name to encompass the many talented performers, as well as anybody who has flitted past us on the television screen, for whatever reason, as long as they have caught the public eye, has come into use. We now have celebrities and the good, or perhaps bad news is that anybody can be a celebrity and you don't even need to be talented to be one.

Within the past few weeks I came across, stuffed inside a cupboard at home, the Spectrum ZX computer, complete with dozens of games, the original of which was my daughter's Christmas present when she was seven. This was a replacement machine, used only a few times and so it is now in my daughter's house and one day we hope to get round to seeing if it still works.

Computer games have come a long way since then, and over the years when I have watched a game being played, I have marvelled and agreed that the graphics get better with each new console, and everything looks more lifelike. I used to love hitting the brick wall on the early games as well as working through puzzles and mazes and the excitement of the car racing. I don't really see a computer game nowadays that doesn't have heads being blown off and blood all around.

I have my mobile phone now which is never very far away, I am a whiz on a word processor, use emails, the internet and generally speaking use technology on a "need/want to know basis", happy to leave everybody else to do likewise.

While planning a trip to the Edinburgh Festival, a few years ago, Monica sent me a text saying there was Wi-fi at the cottage where we would be staying. After reading the message I quickly replied, "sounds great" then after leaving Monica enough time to read my text I wrote again, "What the bloody hell is Wi-Fi?" It had never crossed my mind how to access my internet account away from home as all I knew was that I had a modem, so learning about Wi-Fi made it all become clear. I wonder sometimes how other people keep up so well with new technology as it changes constantly but at least I try not to embarrass myself too much by keeping my eye open to see what is new, to at least be aware of it.

Having arranged to meet my daughter and grandchildren in their local park, some time ago, as I approached I could see she was being shown what looked like holiday photographs on a small screen. I hadn't seen one of these before and not minding showing my ignorance, I asked what it was. I was told it was an Ipad. That puzzled me and I said so because I thought IPads were smaller, more the size of a mobile phone. It was explained to me that the smaller one was an IPod. After giving this new development some thought, I realised the pace at which things were changing.

I've had a mobile phone for about fifteen years now and wouldn't be without it. I can still remember dreaming about having our own phone when I was a girl when we used the one in the red box at the corner of our road. Using the phone box wouldn't have been nearly so bad if it hadn't been out of order so many times when an important call had to be made. There was another box outside the top shop but again, quite often that too would be out of order. Our John now tells me that he and his mates used to stick worms down the penny slot to block it. The worst I ever did was to ring the operator to tell them to get off the line as there was a train coming. I wonder how many such calls the GPO took.

Eddie and I were talking recently about the various social network sites. After listening to me voicing my opinion, Eddie summed up his own thoughts by saying there is one collective name for all of the sites, but I couldn't really print what he said.

Chapter Ten

Home Life

It's Sunday morning and we've just arrived home from early mass at Father Ramsbottom's. John serves as an altar boy and the same thing happened today as last week. Instead of serving communion, Father Ramsbottom walked away, leaving everybody kneeling at the altar, as he seemed to think the mass was over. He's getting a bit confused, the poor man. I hope it's still counted as going to mass today because it wasn't our fault it finished early. Not that I believe in that rubbish about going to hell if you miss mass any more - but just in case. On the Sundays when we don't make it to mass because mum is too busy to organise us, we have to watch a mass on television. I'd much rather go to church than have to sit quietly for an hour but at least if we watch mass on telly, we don't have to starve like we have to before taking Holy Communion. I don't really think watching mass on television counts as attending but then we haven't exactly missed it, just missed going to church.

The smells coming from the kitchen are mouth watering as mum is doing the week's baking while the dinner roasts in the oven. She's also making the Sunday rice pudding which is the best I've ever tasted, made with rice, butter and evaporated milk and baked in the oven to produce a dark brown skin which tastes scrumptious. Mrs Maybury once said how ambrosia was the food of the Gods and how the name has appropriately been given to one brand of tinned rice pudding but mum's is in a different league altogether than the tinned variety.

I've just peeped round the kitchen door to see how dinner is progressing. Julie is helping mum with the baking, the pine table is in the middle of the floor, covered in bowls, rolling pins, flour, sugar and butter, with a giant sized ball of pastry ready for rolling. Mum is singing along to Two Way Family Favourites which is playing on the radio as she chats to Julie about work and boyfriends. I can hear the roasting tin spitting in the oven and as I look, mum is just popping the rice pudding into the oven signalling to me, as it takes about forty five minutes to bake, that's when the dinner will be ready.

Then just as I'm wondering if there's any chance of grabbing a jam butty to keep me going, with both mum and Julie in the kitchen, things have come to a halt as there's a commotion going on upstairs.

All I know is that mum popped up to the bathroom and I heard her stop to speak to John, asking him to tidy his things away when suddenly she screamed out, "What the bloody hell is that doing here?"

I've run upstairs now, fearful that John has brought some creature into the house, which wouldn't be the first time.

All that fuss over nothing. It turns out that the offending object is the result of John's woodwork lessons in school. He says the class were asked to design and make a pencil case just as John could see that there was a funeral being held at St Anne's church, across the road from the school. That gave him an idea and he decided to make one in the shape of a coffin.

It's burning in the stove now and John's in a state of near collapse as he's repeating what mum said to him. He's just said if it has that good an effect he's going to make some more and sell them.

Back to my jam butty. The dinner will be even later now. I wonder if there is any of the strawberry jar leftover from the one we opened yesterday morning for our breakfast toast. It would be nice if it stretched to when I come home from school tomorrow as, being Monday and wash day, tea will be late and as usual I'll be starving. It isn't just me, none of us like wash days. I might have to make do with the plum jam out of the big two pound jar if that's all that's left. When I asked mum why she buys plum jam when it isn't half as nice as strawberry, she said you get twice as much for half the price so I suppose that makes sense and we are lucky to have the strawberry jam as a weekend treat, along with the marmalade and digestive biscuits mum buys. A dip butty is always a good standby to jam, taken from the beef dripping mum cooks the chips in.

We had another burning incident on another Sunday, sometime after the incinerating of the "coffin" but the offending article this time wasn't burned indoors in the kitchen stove. It wasn't that it was too big to fit in the stove or too risky in any way - it was just that it was something mum said had to be removed from the house immediately and we wouldn't be able to eat our dinner, which was just about ready, until it had been destroyed, in the garden, in a fire mum purposely lit inside the garden bin.

We watched mum from the dining table, all of us doubled up laughing, with a look on her face that would befit an exorcism, as a copy of "Playboy" disappeared into the flames, being the property of one of the boys.

Sundays spent at home, as long as I had somewhere good to go on the Monday, could be the happiest times but they could be spoilt at the prospect of school on a Monday at other times.

Mondays were mum's wash days which I found depressing if I walked in from school, hungry, to find mum still had the wash boiler and mangle in the middle of the kitchen floor, steaming the windows up. There'd be water dripping everywhere from the washing as well as condensation dripping down the walls, windows and mum who looked fit to drop, with wisps of damp hair trailing down from her turban. My early memories of mum are of when she had black hair with one grey streak which I would watch her trying to fix in the mirror sometimes, saying the grey streak was "dead".

It was easier to dry the washing in the summer as the clothes could be dried on the garden line, of course, but still there would be piles of wet washing stacked on the draining boards in a queue for drying space. One of those Victorian ceiling pulleys for drying clothes would have come in very handy, in place of the one piece of washing line we had over the kitchen sink, in the hope of catching the heat from the boiler. We also had one wooden clothes maiden which we placed in front of the fire. I really don't know how mum managed to get everything dry but she must have wrung every drop of water out with that mangle. For emergency drying she would place newspaper over the oven door, light the gas oven on a low heat and put the wet clothes on top. This worked quite well, with the washing drying in a similar way to putting it on radiators today although we did have to watch the clothes didn't scorch, giving rise to a toasted smell.

Prior to this of course the clothes had to be washed and this lengthy process involved the use of the wash boiler, to which Mum would add a "dolly blue" whitener for the whites. The dolly blue was a concoction of baking soda and blue colour to help in the whitening process. It came in a little mesh bag tied at the top, resembling the shape of a bunch of garlic cloves.

Dad wore a white shirt with detachable collars, allowing the shirt to be worn more than once with a fresh collar each day, attached by the means of studs. The collars would be dipped in starch after washing and when dry and ironed, they would be fresh and crisp. I once volunteered to do the starching and ironing as I liked messing about with starch. I spent ages, using loads of starch to get dad's collars pristine, with a crease like a knife, before proudly showing the finished result to dad, as I stood back to see the look of delight on his face. Instead of the praise I was expecting, he took one look at the collars and asked me if I was trying to cut his bloody throat, they were that stiff.

I never offered to starch the collars again but made use of the starch for my own purposes, such as on the net underskirts we wore around the time I was about twelve. Having made up the starch solution by adding the powder to water, I quickly dipped the skirt before leaving it to dry with the desired effect being that it would "stick out" beautifully. The starch powder worked fine but whenever we ran out, it could be substituted by melting sugar in hot water. Using sugar was very much a hit and miss process as not only did it not always work and the material remained limp, even when it did work it could leave a residue of undissolved sugar which would irritate your legs. I found this out one Sunday when I was at mass with Margaret. We were going straight to Formby beach after mass to meet up with some school friends. By the time the mass finished, the pew was covered in sugar and our skirts were limp.

We had some good times on those trips out to Formby, catching the train to Sandhills then out to Formby station where we met up with my school friends from Everton Valley - Ann, Linda and Margaret. We always took a picnic which we ate in style in the station waiting room at Formby with the crockery and cutlery we also brought to set on the table before sitting down to eat, watched over by a portrait of Lord Beeching which stood in the fireplace of the cosy little room. I can vaguely remember that Lord Beeching had fallen from grace with the general public and being aware of the fact, one of my friends once discarded the remains of a can of carnation cream down his portrait, before we scarpered.

After lunch we would have a wander round Formby woods where we often ended up lost with everybody having a different sense of direction, apart from me as that's something I've never really had. In fact I still don't think I've ever found my way round Formby woods as I've always had to rely on other people to find the way out. I was well and truly lost on that last trip I made with Margaret and our school friends as we walked round and round for so long it was turning to dusk. We must have walked miles in the wrong direction until we eventually breathed a sigh of relief as we came across a big, old, rambling house which backed on to wherever we were. We could see that there was somebody at home as a woman started walking towards us, down the long garden. We called out to her, waving and shouting hello and that we were lost, when we saw that she was aiming an air rifle at us. She was obviously scared so we thought we were reassuring her by telling her it was alright, we were on our own, when she raised the gun as if to shoot. I don't know what the woman did next as we didn't hang around to find out, but she didn't shoot. We were all a bit shaken and subdued as we found our way back to the station as we all agreed that we'd gone off

Formby.

I was recalling this story just a few years ago to a work colleague who told me that she had an auntie who lived in that vicinity at the time I was talking about, who kept an air rifle to warn off intruders.

Any trips out with friends or indeed just playing out, were always dependent upon our finishing our jobs as we all had to help out with the chores at home, otherwise mum would have had to work round the clock. Mum spent the best part of fourteen years pregnant, thanks she once told me, to being catholic and listening to the priest threatening hell and damnation from the pulpit each Sunday if contraception was used. She once told me that she had practised "the rhythm method" of birth control eight times but added, as she often did, that she wouldn't have been without any of us. Mum had a lot of pride and earned the respect of the shopkeepers as well as the neighbours who knew us well, some of whom could be seen occasionally delivering a bag of used clothes to the door which mum would politely refuse as we didn't wear second hand cast offs. We were well fed, clean and warm but as I have said earlier, fancy clothes were something we didn't have. Our clothes were handed down within the family but at least they were our own.

During those times of mum's "confinements", we were looked after by various members of the family. I was three and Margaret would be just two when John was born and we were both taken to stay with

Granny who then lived in Douglas Road in Anfield. My only memory of that little episode is crystal clear. I can still see us both sitting together in an armchair in Granny's sitting room, with a fire blazing in the grate. We were each holding a bowl of rice pudding and discussing what to do with it as we didn't want to eat it and didn't want to tell Granny, who I remember as being very gentle and kind and we didn't want to upset her. We decided to get rid of the rice by throwing it on the fire thinking it would burn away and we were surprised, as was Granny when she came back into the room, at the sight of the watery mess spluttering away over the coals.

Just eighteen months later it was Monica's turn to be born and again with Margaret, I went to stay with Auntie Margaret and Uncle Tom, at the pub they managed at the time, over the water in New Ferry. I was very homesick so it was a bit of a miserable stay. It was during that visit that I had my first cup of coffee, with my breakfast one morning, while sitting with Margaret and my five cousins. At home I drank milk or water so when Auntie Margaret asked if I would like tea or coffee I told her I didn't want either. She was busy and pushed me for an answer so I asked for coffee. I really didn't like the milky drink I was given but Auntie Margaret said I'd asked for it so had to drink it. It took me about an hour to drink, sitting there on my own, aged four and a half, missing my mummy.

Trips to the pub generally over the following years were a treat. Auntie Margaret and Uncle Tom were very kind even if they did treat us like the poor relations.   Their living accommodation was above the pubs they managed which changed and went more upmarket over the years from Rock Ferry, through New Ferry, Moreton to their last one in West Kirby.   Uncle Tom would always head down to the bar as soon as we arrived, to return laden with pop and crisps.

Sheila was born twenty months after Monica and this time Auntie Margaret came to stay with us as her own children were past the baby stage and uncle Tom could manage without her. By this time I had just turned seven and I missed mum terribly but didn't tell anybody. I barely spoke a word all the time mum was away and overheard Auntie Margaret telling dad she thought I must be ill.   Poor dad, I suppose I looked ok to him and a quiet child would be the least of his worries as his eighth child was born. Auntie Margaret did her best to help and in an effort to cheer me up one freezing cold morning, as it was in January when Sheila was born, she told me she had a special treat for tea. I knew mum was due home the following day and coupled with the prospect of a treat for tea, I skipped off to school happily. All day long I speculated about what would be for tea, visualising chocolate cakes dripping with icing, like mum made.   It turned out that my idea of a treat was quite different to Auntie Margaret's as I was to discover when she served piping hot plates of mashed potato, liver and onions.

Once the family was complete we worked, or muddled through together, each doing our allotted chores, albeit reluctantly at times.   When dad once asked me to wash up after tea I told him I'd been at work all day and was tired. He said, "Have you now, well you must have worked hellish bloody hard, now get and wash the dishes." Another time when I told him I was bored he said, "Bored? I'll give you bored, get in the kitchen and help your mummy." There were times it was best to lie low and keep your mouth closed.

My tea would be spoilt whenever it was my turn to wash up, at the prospect ahead of scrubbing the greasy pans and plates after a meal for ten people. We had to scrub the pans with wire wool after the liberal use of grease to cook with and to wash the crockery and cutlery we used just hot water, as dad wouldn't allow washing up liquid in the house. It was futile to protest at the lack of any detergent so we just got on with it and laughed even though it was really no joke looking down into a sink with grease floating on top of the water and if there was no hot water in the tank, we had to boil the kettle and pans of water on the stove. The prospect of cleaning up the kitchen after tea may have been daunting but I must say there was always a feeling of satisfaction when it was finished and sometimes I wasn't the only one to get carried away, cleaning the whole room, ending with mopping the floor over until everything was gleaming. Then the next day the whole palaver would be repeated.

The kitchen drain itself would be kept grease free with the tons of washing powder that disappeared down it, thankfully, as even though we did have a bathroom, mum found it quicker and easier to dip us in the kitchen sink as she spent such a lot of time standing there anyway. That was fine when we were babies but by the age of four or five you have a sense of modesty and embarrassment that mum didn't seem to notice. It was bad enough having to stand in the sink which looked out over South Park Road, but mortifying when the postman, coal man or anybody else happened to pass by as we were being scrubbed.

We never left the house in the mornings while we were at St Mary's without a quick visit to stand at the the sink, when mum showed no mercy as she scrubbed our face and neck until almost red raw. We were tough little mites in those days, especially in the winter time, getting up in the freezing cold, without the mollycoddling central heating in today's homes. Not that a bit of cold did us any harm but those walks down Station Road to the bus stop in the mornings weren't much fun at times. The girls wore knee length socks held up with garters made of pieces of thick knicker elastic tied in a knot, while some of the boys wore short trousers, with all of us at one time or another, ending up with chapped skin behind our knees and oh, how it hurt. Rubbing Vaseline onto the affected area helped but constantly walking in the cold and damp held up the healing process.

Warts were something we shared, passing them round to each other which although painless, were unsightly and embarrassing. I had one on the palm of my hand for a long time which I covered with one finger whenever I had to open my hand. The

Iodene we used to treat cold sores by walking round with a purple splodge on our mouths, didn't work on warts. They were something we put up with until they disappeared but I decided one night that I'd had enough of the wart on my hand and hunted round the house for a cure, thinking there must be some way of getting rid of it. I spotted the Ralgex deep heat treatment stick that mum used for various aches and sprains, thinking how strong it smelled and how it burned on the skin. So, I decided it was worth trying to burn my wart off. After daubing my hand with the preparation, I went to sleep and woke up the following morning to find my wart had completely disappeared.

As can be gathered by now, we didn't argue with dad - whatever he said went and that was the end of it. Once his mind was made up there was not much point in trying to argue although I did attempt to at times. He added the word sheen onto each of our names when he wasn't happy with one of us so you would know if you were in trouble as, in my case I would hear him call "Katsheen", Julie was "Jusheen" and so on.

Monica was always very well behaved and it was a rare day the time she dared to defy dad. She'd be about thirteen at the time and as it was getting towards the end of the day, dad noticed she hadn't come in yet and it was her turn to wash up. She was standing just outside the house on the grass verge, talking to her friends, as he asked me to call her in. She looked at me and thought for a couple of seconds and then just said "No." I couldn't believe it, but thought it was hilarious as I went back and told dad. I wanted to see his reaction as this was a "first" from Monica. Dad's reply was typical of him when he said, "Tell her if she doesn't come in now I'll drag her in by the ear". I was splitting my sides as I went outside to repeat it to Monica who by this time was trying to keep face with her friends, so she again refused to come in and well, I have to say that I reported back to dad, again waiting for his reaction. He put down his copy of the Daily Express, stood up and walked towards the door calling "Monsheen" as he went. Once outside he went straight to Monica, took hold of her ear and led her inside with her face the colour of the phone box across the road. Whenever I tried to tell Monica I didn't expect dad to react as he did, and was sorry I'd told on her, she never believed me as she said I had a smirk on my face at the time.

With Sundays spent in the kitchen and Mondays doing the washing, the remainder of mum's week would be spent, like other housewives, doing general housework and cooking. We had a delivery of groceries from the Co-op in Fazakerley on Tuesdays and every Saturday would see Gerry and Eddie taking a huge holdall on the bus, to return with it full. There were times I would groan when I saw mum appear at the door while we were playing outside as more often than not she would ask me and Margaret to go to the Co-op to stock up on supplies.

After one such trip to the Co-op, on the return journey, Margaret and I had three brown paper carrier bags with string handles to carry between us and agreed to take a handle each of the third bag. When we got off the bus back in Kirkby, we agreed to take turns at carrying two bags but couldn't agree on who would carry the second bag first. We were standing arguing on the corner of Glover's Brow and Kirkby Row, about eight minutes walk away from home, holding a bag each with the third one sitting on the ground when I walked off saying Margaret would have to pick it up. She didn't pick it up though and as we both walked home it began to rain, heavily. Neither of us spoke, both thinking the other would give in but my heart was pounding, knowing there was no way we could tell mum what we'd done. We were half way down South Park Road, two minutes from home when we both stopped and looked at each and without a word turned and ran as though our lives depended on it. The bag was still there in a sopping wet heap and mum was none the wiser. We were lucky.

Eddie had the job of delivery boy at the Co-op for a short spell after leaving school. His round would take him out of Fazakerley to the surrounding areas including Kirkby and Simonswood. Eddie was always pleasant and would no doubt have a tale to tell whenever he dropped off his deliveries and was always very generously tipped in return as the customers liked him. He was paid about £4 per week by the Co-op and could make half of this again in tips. He was quite shrewd and clever where his money was concerned and always has been, but at that time he spent his wages well, saving a bit once he had paid mum for his keep but any tips he made, he gave straight to mum, saying he had all he needed.

The Co-op operated a Dividend system, known to everybody as "divvy". I have it from Eddie that mum's dividend number was 209175. Each time a customer paid they were allocated a token and periodically they received a payment in exchange, as a share of the profits. Mr Parkinson was the shop manager and whenever I called in I was greeted with a smile as I handed over mum's shopping list as he said he was going to buy mum a typewriter one day.

We paid cash for everything of course, as that is how the money came home. The Co-op had a pulley system which involved the shop assistant taking your cash and locking it into a small box attached to an overhead pulley. It would then be sent off to a cash office on a higher level somewhere in the building to be returned a few minutes later with any change due, all of which I found fascinating to watch.

The amount to be paid off the Co-op account would be determined by mum and dad "balancing the budget" each Thursday night, dad's pay day, after we had all gone to bed. They would shut themselves in the front room with a pot of tea and dad would empty his pay packet. Between them they would apportion dad's wages, working out whatever was due for payment and what was to be bought. When they had finished, a row of coins would be stacked along the mantelpiece above the fire, the amounts decreasing according to our ages. This was our weekly pocket money.

We bought most of our meat from Mr Granby, the butcher who parked his van in the road every Tuesday afternoon. After weighing out whatever we asked for, he would always throw an extra chop or a few sausages on top, and wink as he wrapped it up. He was a gentleman.

Dad brought fish and chips in on his way home on Thursday nights, which was a highlight of our week. Chip portions came in two sizes at a cost of either four or six old pence and as well as battered cod, the shop sold fish cakes the likes of which I haven't seen or tasted in years. If you ask for a fish cake in a chip shop these days you're likely to be sold a thin slice of breadcrumbs with barely enough filling to taste, rather than a big fat fish and potato mix covered in thick batter and fried in lard. They were absolutely delicious and I would go a long way today to taste another one. The chip shop also sold "scallops" which were sliced potato fried in batter. Not much went to waste in those days and for a penny you could buy a bag of left over batter which would taste of fish but I don't think that was over popular, mainly being bought by children out playing, with a spare penny in their pocket. Whatever was bought went into greaseproof paper bags before being wrapped in old newspapers donated by customers, which we didn't think twice about using.

After tea, the chip bags would then be filled with an assortment of sweets bought by dad from the top shop on his way home from work. I will love fish and chips forever.

North Sea Gas reached Kirkby in 1966. Prior to that, coal gas had been used in the home and although existing gas appliances could be used for the new, natural gas, British Gas were offering such a good discount on a new cooker that most people on the estate bought a new one. A temporary office was set up at the end of our road while the works were ongoing. A free gift was issued with every cooker, being a run of the mill set of baking trays with every standard cooker bought, or a set of good quality saucepans with the deluxe model.

Mum had an appointment in town that day and everyone was out either at school or work apart from Monica and I who were briefed to ensure the installation of our new cooker went smoothly, which it did, complete with the baking trays inside the oven. Finding ourselves at a loose end for the rest of the day, we hatched a plan which involved Margaret calling to tell the people in the office that they were supposed to have included a set of the nice saucepans and not the baking trays they had left by mistake. We knew that Margaret, always very confident, would have no problem in stating her case. As soon as she arrived home from work we told her the story and watched as she went, "on the bounce", to tear a strip off the men as she handed the trays back to them. Monica and I watched her walking back as we hid behind the privet hedge in the front garden. She was laughing but saying something about killing us.

We paid for our gas supply by putting shilling pieces, the pre-decimal equivalent of five pence, into a gas meter, housed in a tiny cupboard under the stairs. The meter would then be emptied periodically by an employee from the Gas Board calling to the house. The amount due to pay for the gas used would be calculated and there was always a considerable refund given to mum which came as a good bonus to her.

As I have said, fashion was something that we didn't come close to while still at school although it was different when we were little as we didn't have to follow any style. As girls, we wore our hair either in bunches or plaits with half a yard of ribbon tied in a bow at each end or on Sundays and special occasions the ribbon would be tied in a huge bow, on top of our heads. For the boys, haircuts were strictly "short back and sides", although John had been hankering for a crew cut for some time at around the age of thirteen. Dad sent him down to the barbers in Melling one afternoon for his usual cut but when he came back dad, who was in bed as he was working the night shift, sent him back to the barbers to cut more off, saying it was a "come again" cut. John didn't need telling twice as he headed off happily to the barbers, to return with his crew cut, asking dad if it was short enough. All dad could say was, "You've got a head like a bloody turnip."

Eddie swears that mum used to cut dad's old trousers down for him to wear to school and that he once had to wear a pair of dad's old boots. I think he's exaggerating but he remains adamant. Gerry says there was a time when boys would be skitted for wearing brown shoes so when dad bought him a pair, quite possibly because they were cheap but good quality, he dyed them black and Gerry was skitted all the more for wearing brown shoes dyed black. Children can be cruel. John wasn't left out when the shoes were brought in by dad as he took delight in the Army type pair dad once bought for him, which John referred to as his "kebbers".

One of the biggest pains of my formative years was the shoes I had to wear. From when I was twelve the fashion in footwear was for "casuals", a dainty shoe with a dainty heel which made going to school almost bearable the day mum bought me a pair when I was thirteen. I'd also just been allowed to start wearing nylons instead of socks so felt quite grown up. I loved those shoes but the heels wore down very quickly compared to the heavy duty clodhoppers I was used to wearing and after being repaired about three times dad, not mum, went out and bought me a pair of brown brogues to wear for school. The school regulation stipulated black shoes so a bottle of "Lady Esquire" black shoe dye was duly purchased to transform them. The dye had a very distinctive smell which lasted for days until it wore off and the black dye had a blue tinge so had to be covered with black shoe polish when dry. I must admit that once this process was complete, you couldn't tell that the shoes had been dyed unless you looked underneath to see where the dye went over the edge. I lay awake crying for the whole of one Sunday night, dreading going to school to be humiliated. As it turned out the other girls were sympathetic but they did look a bit puzzled as to why I had to wear the shoes, especially when one of them spotted the dye underneath and saw that they weren't even black to start with. Maybe they understood a bit more than I realised as after all, most of us were not all that well off.

Mine weren't the worst pair of shoes dad ever bought for us as the ones he came home with for Margaret one day were, well, hard to believe, and it really was quite unfair to expect her to wear them. They were black with a suede type upper and a doorstep sized sole and heel formed out of rubber. Margaret didn't say a lot when dad handed her the shoes but then she would know there was no point in arguing. Some time later I picked one of the shoes up from the bedroom floor to see that the heel was missing and the shoe was stuffed with newspaper. Margaret and I fell about laughing when I asked her questions like what she did when it rained and she said she changed the newspaper or when we went to communion and had to kneel at the altar and she said she let the shoes slip off so whoever was behind her couldn't see. After an argument with Margaret shortly afterwards I went and told mum all about the shoes. I did feel guilty afterwards for snitching but at least Margaret never had to wear the shoes again.

Mum did understand our feelings of peer pressure most of the time but she did sometimes agree with dad, saying we had too much false pride. I never knew the difference between pride and false pride myself. I had worn a grey gabardine mac as my outdoor uniform while at Everton Valley, which was virtually new when I left, having been made to last forever, as reflected in the price. As I was leaving for college one morning in the pouring rain, mum told me to wear the mac. I thought she was joking as I told her I wouldn't be seen dead in it, before I realised that she was serious. No amount of sobbing would make any difference as mum stood her ground telling me it was a perfectly good mac and my pleading that I would be a laughing stock at the college made no difference. I had to go to college that day as it was exam time and I left the house breaking my heart. As mum closed the door behind me I had a brainwave and taking the offending mac off, I threw it in the shed. I think mum had forgotten all about it when I went home and never mentioned it again.

Of all our neighbours, the Boltons were probably the ones we knew best. We all got on really well and they never complained about noise or anything else for that matter. Mrs Bolton was more down to earth than her husband and like mum, she would often give you a knowing look, as if she had you completely weighed up.

There was, however, one glaring difference between the two families, quite apart from our lifestyles, and that was religion. While we weren't extreme in our beliefs, being average Catholics, the Boltons practised their own religion devoutly, especially Mr Bolton. I was aware I was a Catholic from the age of three and can remember a discussion I had with Pauline while we were playing in our back garden at the time. Because of my name, with my childish logic, I was insisting that girls were Catholic so boys must be Protestant but Pauline was equally insistent that she was neither. Whenever I asked her over the years what religion they were, she was always evasive and the closest I ever got to an answer was that they were "Believers". Their place of worship was somewhere in Walton, where they went twice every Sunday. Neither Pauline nor her elder sister were allowed out of doors on Sundays apart from going to church and we weren't even allowed to speak if we saw them leaving the house.

I don't know what gave me the idea that Mr Bolton was above reproach but it was possibly because most conversations I had with him would include the topic of God. Added to that, Pauline had repeated her dad's views on swearing being sinful so I spent some time like a bundle of nerves, not wanting dad to be within earshot while we were playing, in case they heard him swear. Not that he ever uttered an obscenity. His glossary of swearwords was made up of a core of the same few words which he would amend or jumble up to suit the occasion producing such words as "buggeroo" prefixed by "stupid".

While we were playing in the garden one Saturday afternoon, I heard, loud and clear through an open window, dad saying "damn". I was mortified and blabbed to Pauline, "Isn't it strange how you can mishear people sometimes, like just then for instance when my dad said "darn", it sounded for all the world like "damn." Being Catholic wasn't easy at times, meeting sin on every corner.

Mr Bolton took every opportunity to "spread the word" about God to whoever would listen and as children, we were a captive audience. I have no doubt that a discussion about religion would have taken place between him and dad in the past, just the once. Whenever dad saw Mr Bolton talking to us he would say he hoped he hadn't been bible punching which was indeed often the case, although we never admitted it. Mr Bolton joined in a game we were playing of throwing a ball around outside the houses one evening, taking the opportunity to talk about Jesus. I could see dad watching through the front room window so was panicking in case he came out to hear the "God chat" but when I saw that he was laughing as he must have been telling mum what was going on, I could relax.

Dad taught Auntie Maureen to drive and she bought herself a little car after passing her test. The first time she drove up to our house on a Sunday afternoon, dad saw her approaching the house and called through the window, "Bloody hell Maureen, I told you to park outside, not in the front room." He wasn't the best person to inspire confidence in a new driver. I used to go out with him when he was teaching Gerry and Eddie to drive and can remember once when I chipped in from the back seat, being asked if I wanted to "bloodywell get out and walk", from Fazakerley. So when Mr Bolton expressed an interest in learning to drive and dad offered to teach him, we were all a bit unsure. They got on very well together generally and would often help each other out but it was just dad's opinion of any other driver, let alone a learner, that worried us, as well as the language problem.

Mr Bolton's lessons took place on summer evenings, lasting about an hour each time, with dad reporting back that Mr Bolton was progressing well. Then one night dad came back after being out for only about fifteen minutes. Mum called to him from the kitchen asking why he was home early. I knew exactly what she was thinking because I was thinking the same. She said she hoped he hadn't sworn at Mr Bolton. Dad just said that everything was fine as he laughed quietly. Mr Bolton completed his lessons and passed his test but with a different instructor.

Another of our friendly neighbours was Mrs Alsop, who succeeded the Bartons at the corner shop when they sold it in the late 1960s. This was after the shop changed hands a couple of times but did eventually go to Mrs Alsop, who lived with her husband in one of the private houses at the top of South Park Road. It was Mrs Alsop who gave Monica her first Saturday job. There wasn't much of a need for help in the shop but I think Mrs Alsop was glad of the company. She was very kind and I think she thought of Monica as a daughter as she had married quite late in life and didn't have children of her own.

We were never quite sure why they bought the shop but it seemed to be more of a hobby than a business venture and it wasn't run very well. The supermarkets had affected the trade of the corner shops but there was still a need for them and indeed the Campbell's shop continued to thrive. Mrs Alsop's stock would run very low or run out altogether and was never replenished as it should have been, resulting in customers walking in to half empty shelves in the mornings. Whenever Monica was working and a customer asked for something they didn't have, Mrs Alsop would tell them it would be in later in the day if they would like to call back. She would then send Monica up to Campbell's shop to buy whatever was required. Mrs Campbell knew what was going on and would ask Monica if she was shopping for the shop.

We came by a ouija board from Mrs Alsop which had been loaned to her by her next door neighbour whose husband had banned it from their house. The board, which was expensive looking and made out of wood, with the letters and numbers cleared etched out, was sub loaned to Monica. On the two or three occasions we used it, no spirits surfaced so I tried to liven things up one night by spelling out that somebody was going to die. Gerry heard screams, burst into the room, took hold of the board and broke it over his knee. We tried to replace it but couldn't find where they were sold, so it was left to Monica to explain to Mrs Alsop why she couldn't return the board.

Whenever I have been asked where I come from, telling people I'm from Kirkby is nothing more than a bit of background information to most people but there are always some people who make something of an issue of it. A girl I once worked with in a Solicitors' office couldn't quite get her head round why I don't have a broad Liverpool accent, while one of the solicitors contributed to the conversation by stating that, "All people who live in Kirkby are thick". As it happened, he was a really nice man and it just goes to show how a degree of ignorance can prevail in people. When I reminded him of my origins he replied that I had left Kirkby and that he meant the people who still live there. I have been asked what the people of Kirkby are like and always answer quite simply that we are the same as people from anywhere else, we are all different. I usually ask the person asking the question when they were last in Kirkby and the usual answer is that they have never been. Monica was once offered a lift home by a college friend who drove as far as Fazakerley, then dropped her off as she refused to enter Kirkby.

We found our own way of dealing with unwanted questioning as Margaret did one night on her way home from work. While sitting at Exchange Station she was chatted up by a man asking her a lot of questions about where she lived, who with etc. She told him she was an only child, the daughter on an accountant and lived in West Kirby on the Wirral, in a large detached house and she was going home to check on the horses. After chatting for ten minutes and as the Kirkby train pulled in she told him she would have to go as this was her train.

The evenings when we were all at home were very special, looking back. When we were younger we would sit round the table with mum and dad to play board games such as Lotto or Housey Housey. I liked playing cards best when dad taught us games like Rummie, Old Maid or Tuppence Ha'penny where we gambled for matchsticks.

We were all quite young when we lost dad who died after a long battle with cancer, but something he said a few years before he died, stayed with me and became an unquestionable source of comfort some years later. I was listening to my beloved Radio Caroline on my pink transistor radio one afternoon while dad was pottering around quietly. *Single Girl* by Sandy Posey was playing at the time as dad interrupted my listening to say quite simply, "I like this song". I was surprised, being more used to hearing him call all pop songs a noise and there were none of them he would listen to if they were being played live in the back garden.

Dad died fifteen years before mum and during those years in between, I heard the song played on the radio occasionally, maybe once every year or so. Each time I heard it I would stop and think, "I wonder why dad said he liked this song."

I believe I had my answer when, at twenty past eleven one April morning, as I was listening to Jimmy Young on Radio 2, the song started playing, just as the phone rang out. I walked from my kitchen to answer the phone, thinking as I walked through, "Oh well, I'll never know now why dad said he liked this song." The telephone call was from Julie who had just arrived at mum's house to see an ambulance driving slowly away. We had lost mum as she had died suddenly.

Chapter Eleven

Kirkby Ghosts

Most of us like a good ghost story. I haven't known many people who haven't been prepared to listen to a tale even if after hearing it they dismiss it as rubbish. After listening to one such tale on the radio one afternoon I was repeating it to a confirmed sceptic friend, telling her how red flames attracted the spirits and I'd just had to turn the "Magicoal" log effect fire off. She listened then said, "You do realise don't you that I'm going to be on my own in this house tonight?" I said I didn't think she'd be bothered because she didn't believe in ghosts anyway to which she replied, "Well I think it's a load of crap but I'm not certain". Similarly, an atheist boss I once had, after telling a white lie to a client, turned to me saying he would never go to heaven. When I asked how that would be possible when he didn't believe there was any such place he said, "Just in case". I have never spoken to anybody in person who has told me that they believe categorically that life ends with death, but of course lots of us have doubts.

I have never to my knowledge seen a ghost, for which I can't say I'm sorry. I do, however, firmly believe in the supernatural. This isn't any sort of considered opinion, it's just an innate awareness. From an early age the subject of ghosts fascinated me, my interest developing to looking for explanations rather than white floating spirits.

Scientific research talks of residual energy remaining from events that have taken place in the past and being recorded in certain conditions in carbon or rust and I'm sure there is a quote in the Bible somewhere about "walls holding secrets" but unfortunately I can't recall the details. The more I hear that can be scientifically explained, the more sceptical I could become, but not everything can be explained away.

I have heard other people's ghost stories, of course, and will relate the Kirkby stories here. As they could be called "hearsay", not being from my own experience, I'm as sceptical as anybody else as to their validity, but I do err on the side of belief, especially of the first one.

This was told to me by a work colleague from the non believer category. Her name is Janet and this was how I came to hear her story.

There were about eight of us sitting at our desks at work one day when somebody mentioned the name of a medium she would like to see. All of us apart from Janet were quite enthusiastic and we agreed to see if we could book an appointment with him. Janet, who hadn't joined in the conversation, carried on working, glancing up at me to say, "You don't believe in all that rubbish do you?" When I said it was just a bit of fun she dismissed it totally and said how stupid we all were. That put a bit of a dampener on things but enquiries were made of the medium who it turned out no longer did private readings as he had made a name for himself and was now fully occupied touring and making television shows.

A few weeks later at work again, the conversation turned to spooky matters - to ghosts this time. None of us had any first hand experience and I looked at Janet, guessing what she was thinking as I said, "I suppose you think this is all a load of rubbish don't you?" I was taken aback when she replied, "Well no, actually I've seen a ghost." She went on to tell us quite matter of factly of how when she lived in Tower Hill in Kirkby she and a friend were walking to the Pear Tree Inn, about a mile out of Kirkby on Prescot Road, past the remaining Kirkby fields. They both saw a spirit like figure become visible from behind a hedge. The figure seemed to float around the field. Bear in mind the fact that they both saw the figure and they hadn't had a drink as they were on their way to the pub rather than away from it. Janet said they were so frightened that they ran the rest of the way to the pub where they told everybody they had just seen a ghost.

It was a busy night in the pub, being close to Christmas with a lot of the regulars being in, who all looked at each other warily and then started to bombard the girls with questions while they stood looking from face to face. It transpired that there had been many reported sightings amongst the locals who all thought they were winding each other up, but once they were convinced the girls were telling the truth, they all visibly paled. I never asked Janet why she thought we were stupid to talk of mediums when she was the only one to have seen a ghost.

The field where Janet and her friend saw the ghost would have been known only to me amongst our colleagues as I knew the area. Part of the field remains as farmland today but some has been developed into a housing estate. I think the sighting would have been across the road from the pub, somewhere around Back Lane, Melrose Road and Galston Close, in Kirkby.

Hauntings in the fields of Kirkby

My next story was told to me by Marie who works in

Kirkby, who in turn was told the story recently by a teacher friend from one of the local schools. Marie would have no reason to doubt the teacher's word, although she herself professes to be a sceptic.

The teacher at the time of her story had been qualified and working in the school for about two years and would quite often spend time in her classroom on her own after the children had gone home. There would be one or two people around including the caretaker, but the building would be quiet of course, and would perhaps take on an eerie feeling, especially when it was dark in the wintertime. Even allowing for this, the teacher was telling Marie how every time she was on her own in her classroom, she felt as if she wasn't alone, and could feel a presence. She went with friends to visit a medium for the first time, for no other reason than having an open minded interest.   The medium, however, told her there were two ladies whose names both began with the letter M, who were watching over her in her workplace.

Marie immediately thought of the "presence" she had felt in school. She was aware that at least one past teacher from the school had died but didn't know her name. After enquiring at the school, she was told that two teachers whose names both began with the letter M had died within the past ten years.

I have never to my knowledge ever seen a ghost but that doesn't mean I haven't seen one unknowingly. This story is one of my own which possibly bears out that theory. As a child in Kirkby, I regularly went with friends and my sisters on bike rides in and around Kirkby and occasionally rode out to Simonswood. This was mainly only when there was a gang of us going together as it was quite a way from home and we could be liable to get lost. Apart from that, Simonswood was quite isolated and as such not the ideal place to play. The boys scared us with the stories handed down by the people of Kirkby, of the Kirkby witches who had apparently inhabited the area for over a hundred years. Legend had it that it was to Simonswood they were taken after being tried and condemned to be burnt at the stake and there is allegedly, a burnt out tree stump said the be the place of execution for the poor unfortunate women.

Pauline and I were out on our bikes one day on our own when we went too far and ended up at Simonswood, quite lost. We rode around trying to find the right road home but seemed to be going round in circles. We hadn't seen a soul, with or without a body, for miles, and then eventually we saw a woman standing by the side of the road. With relief we cycled up to her, calling out as we approached that we were lost. The woman looked pleasant enough and as we drew closer to her we could see she was practically dressed in rags. She didn't answer us at all - she just stared, smiling. Having come to the conclusion that she must be deaf, we gave up asking directions and as we needed to find the way home, we rode off, found the right road and headed for home. I was curious about the woman though and asked Pauline if perhaps she was lost herself. We stopped to look back before leaving the road but again, there was nobody in sight. I told everyone later how we had got lost and that the only person we saw to ask for directions turned out to be deaf, in an attempt to reassure myself.

Gerry's wife, Jean, tells a story about Waverley House. There are more than likely dozens of tales of hauntings of the building but Jean says she witnessed this one herself. As mentioned earlier on my walk round the estate, Waverley House is a big, old spooky looking house where I spent time ghost hunting when I was little. Gerry, by his own admission, has spent more time than a lot of people in the building but that is mainly due to him being on the committee for a while and sleeping over on occasions. He says the only spirits he ever saw came out of bottles.

I've heard vague stories over the years about a nanny by the name of Mrs Watson who is said to have haunted the house since her untimely death in the 1940s or 50s, and this is Jean's story.

It was after she went behind the bar to help out one evening on a busy night, that the conversation turned to Mrs Watson, when one of the regulars to the club, Doris Peters, said she'd just seen Mrs Watson standing outside the ladies' room, as large as life. Mrs Peters said she saw the spirit on most of her visits to the club, wandering round, but never speaking. In the light of what Mrs Peters said, Jean along with some of her friends decided to hold a seance once the customers had all left, using a makeshift ouija board. Anybody who has taken part in this, not to be recommended pastime, will no doubt be familiar with the feeling of trepidation and excitement mixed with thinking it's "just a laugh", especially after you've had a drink or two. Many people will also be familiar with what happens next, that is - nothing happens in the majority of cases - but not all, or so I have been told. The participants were asking random questions to thin air, having each placed a finger on a glass. The glass didn't move in response to any of their many questions for some time but it did eventually, according to Jean, fly into the air and shatter into pieces. Gerry was in another room at the time so didn't witness anything and when told, said they'd all had too much to drink but according to Jean, she was quite sober and they couldn't all have imagined the shattered glass.

I doubt if any of these stories will have scared anybody and unless you happen to live within the vicinity of the roads near the Pear Tree Inn, then you won't need to sleep with the lights on.

Before I finish on the subject of ghostly goings on I would just like to say that I did get to see the medium I talked about earlier, at one of his shows. I had asked Monica did she want to come along and she was undecided, being the sceptic. I remembered a few days before the show and checked online to find there were just a few tickets left on the back row of the theatre. I was at work at the time so sent Monica a text asking her had she made her mind up as there were only a few tickets left. She did reply that she would go and told me later that at the time the text came through she was teaching her class of seven years olds as they were discussing different forms of communication such as letters, telephone and emails. As she was talking, she heard her mobile alert and said, "And of course you can send a message by text, like the one that's just coming through to me". She opened my message asking did she want to see the medium.

On the evening of the show we arrived at the theatre and I believed I was going to see the best medium in the business. I had watched one or two others but still had to be convinced. One show I went to was too good to be true. There were two groups of people sitting separately in the back row, on either side of the room, who received messages from the spirit world. One of the groups had lost a family member in tragic circumstances. I watched the people and it looked to me that either they had heard it all before and it was nothing new to them or else they had been planted in the audience. I actually heard one of the women saying she was bored. During the show the audience was asked if there was a lady present whose husband had died on his way home from the pub on a Friday night. About eight women put their hands up.

Back to the show, during which I was sure that I was going to see some evidence of "the other side" and that Monica would be converted, as she said she had an open mind. I'm not sure about Ian, her husband, as he loves a good ghost story as much as I do but is non committal as to how much he believes as he usually laughs them off. The last thing I expected was to find it funny enough to make me cry with laughter or that I would have trouble staying awake, both of which happened.

It was during one of the mini heat waves we have sometimes in May and the theatre was extremely hot. The show started off well and when the medium first walked on stage looking every inch the showman, he looked up at the back row, straight at us, which was very exciting and had me thinking, "Oh my God, this is it, he's got a message for us", but unfortunately he moved on to two people in the row in front of us. He seemed to be working his way towards the front of the audience as the show progressed and I was surprised at how many of the names from previous generations were visiting from the other side, such as Albert, Gladys and Maud.

The show started to get predictable and boring and with the warmth of the theatre plus the couple of drinks we had had in the foyer, it was then that I started to feel drowsy and had to shake myself to stay awake. I was concentrating on the names of people in the audience who had "visits", while listening out for our names. I turned to Monica and said, "You know, of the few hundred women here there will be a fair few with variations of my name, Katherine, Kathleen, Kate etc., so if one of those names is called it won't be anything to get excited about. If there is a message for "Monica", though, the chances are it could be for you."

Monica replied, "Yes, but there won't be any other Katsheens will there?"

It was at that point that things started to fall apart and we began to see the funny side, which our host helped along with his next and final visitation. He said he was looking for a man named John who would be sitting towards the front of the theatre, on the left side. He found John easily enough, sitting about three rows from the front. When John was asked to confirm that he was looking to buy a new car he replied that he had had his car for five years, just had the MOT passed and he had no plans to replace the car. The medium persisted, possibly trying not to lose face, by asking John had he been looking at car magazines. John said he hadn't looked at any magazines. By this time the show had only about ten minutes to run and people started to leave the theatre, so we followed suit and left while the medium was still on stage, heading for the bar. I decided I had seen all I needed to and have never felt inclined to visit another such show, but I would if I heard of somebody who was said to be genuine.......

Chapter Twelve

Fashion and Socialising

One spring morning while I was working at the Probation Office, one of my colleagues, Barbara, said to me as she put her newspaper down, "We're going to have some fun this year aren't we?" When I asked her what she meant she elaborated by saying as she laughed, how all the young girls would be wearing mini skirts and we would see some sights this year. Barbara was thirty six at the time, while I was sixteen and I thought to myself, "Yes, and I'm going to be one of those sights and I can't wait."

As with each new generation, we were ready to experience and embrace the fashions of the day. Styles come and go, sometimes to return in a modified version, but the mini skirt was radical - and we wore it first.

Since I was fourteen I had worn, and continued to wear dresses and coats 39 inches long, resting sedately at two inches below the knee. As I glimpsed the exciting times ahead, I realised the transition would take a bit of getting used to as well as some planning. My particular problem was how to suddenly start wearing a skirt seven inches shorter than usual without dad noticing. With that thought ever present at the back of my mind I headed off to C & A Modes' bargain basement in Church Street one lunch hour shortly afterwards, with Sharon, to buy my first mini dress. I selected a pale blue collarless and sleeveless dress from the rows of dresses and skirts of all descriptions on the £1.00 rails. The matching skirts and jackets we wore to work at the time, or "costumes" as we called them, were now made with the shorter skirts. Although Sharon wasn't buying a mini herself, she gave me every encouragement, telling me how everyone would be wearing them soon and how her mum had said as soon as she lost weight then she could have one. Sharon put up with her mum's endless quest for her to lose weight and didn't seem particularly bothered herself, as she was very pretty with flaxen coloured hair and never short of a boyfriend. I realised that, being on the tall side, the minis would be even shorter on me and as I tried the dress on I was busy working on my plan.

The first thing I decided was to take the hem down as another three quarters of an inch would make me feel much more comfortable as well as standing a chance of passing for decent in dad's eyes. I lengthened the dress, which left the hemline looking a bit unfinished but at four inches above the knee it could be considered respectable and dad surely couldn't say I looked like a brazen hussy. I worked out that I could wear the dress to work the following day and change out of it when I came home, before dad saw me. Mum was fine about the dress, having better things to worry about, but she did warn me that dad would have something to say when he saw it, as I heard her laughing quietly.

A couple of weeks later, after popping back to C & A's basement my confidence had increased although

I had discovered that one of the prices to be paid for looking so good was the slight loss of dignity as the normal everyday things such as getting on a bus or bending to pick something up could involve degrees of contortion. Nylons held up with suspender belts had by now, of course, been banished to the bin having been replaced with tights which I welcomed, as apart from it being impractical to wear short skirts over nylons, gone were the days of having to stick a coin or a button in a broken suspender belt, along with the worry of your nylons falling down. There were, however, times when no matter how careful you were, somebody would tell you what colour knickers you were wearing because unlike the opaque tights or leggings worn today, our tights were fifteen to thirty denier nylon and as such, were see through.

So by this time, I had decided to give up on having to dodge dad all the time as I became more lax, so much so that I didn't bother getting changed when he was due home one day, thinking he would be so used to seeing mini skirts that he wouldn't bat an eyelid. I got that wrong. While I was sitting minding my own business watching television, I jumped when I heard, "Katsheen, just what the bloody hell do you think you are wearing and where's the other half of that frock? Have you been out of the house like that?" I tried hard to maintain nonchalance as I replied with as much defiance as I dared, determined to stand my ground, "Yes, I wore it to work today. Everyone's wearing them."

After several battles things settled down and dad did

eventually accept us wearing the short skirts and even hot pants when they arrived on the fashion scene. Trousers were not yet acceptable office wear although hot pants or shorts were considered respectable enough, worn over our "American tan" shade of tights, as we never went bare legged. Whatever garb we experimented with, we thought we looked great, as I'm sure we did. Boutiques such as Miss Selfridge, Chelsea Girl and Biba now lined the high streets as the twin sets and A line skirts disappeared to make way for the magical new styles.

Margaret walked in one day having bought a lovely silver lurex, bare midriff dress comprising of a separate bodice and micro mini skirt, held together with metal rings each about three inches in diameter. We discussed how she was going to get round dad and even mum for that matter, as the dress was a bit revealing, and we had to get it passed as decent. Mum presented us with a solution herself when she picked the dress up and asked Margaret what it was. Glancing over to me, Margaret answered mum telling her that it was a dress. Mum replied, "I take it you will be wearing a vest under it?" Margaret reassured her by saying that of course she would wear a vest and the following Saturday night she left the house in an ensemble of the glittery new dress worn over a pink stretchy vest. She put on her coat, said goodbye then went into the coal shed to remove the vest.

There were perks to be had from wearing a mini skirt. Before the days of the "one man buses", the conductors never took bus fare from the nurses travelling to Walton and Fazakerley hospitals on the No 92 bus and that rule was quite often extended to a girl in a mini skirt.

The mid calf length skirt or "midi" as it was known, followed the mini, and then came the long, hippie style maxis. Straight legged cotton "slacks" and jeans disappeared in place of "bell bottoms" which became the only style to wear. Together, designers such as Mary Quant, Biba and Twiggy, the world's first ever supermodel, showed us how good we could look, if we had the confidence to believe in ourselves.

Footwear was also revolutionised during the 60s as women's stylish boots appeared for the first time, the only boots having been worn by women prior to this, were to protect against the bad weather, bearing no resemblance to a fashion accessory. My own favourite clothes from the 60s era were a pair of knee length, white lace boots with a white patent leather shoe, which I wore with red hot pants and a white seersucker blouse. I also had a green pvc coat which I wore over my mini skirts to complete the look. A pair of air force blue suede shoes with a small wedge heel are also in my memory cupboard but it was a scarlet coloured pvc mini skirt, belonging to Monica which was the nicest piece of clothing I think we had between us at that time.

I never did quite work out whether being referred to as a Dolly Bird was intended as a compliment or an insult. The dictionary definition for the term is "A woman who is considered attractive and fashionable but not very clever." That is definitely insulting as well as being untrue as there were girls who always had the right look, in dress, shoes, hair, make up and face and I can't see what isn't clever about that. So, to be referred to as a dolly bird, just occasionally, meant that you had got everything right, if only for the day, and a compliment I gratefully accepted.

The man made fabric used in the manufacture of our clothes, such as crimplene and bri-nylon, although practical in some ways, such as for ease of washing and ironing, were not always comfortable or flattering to wear as they were full of static and too clingy. An underskirt helped to an extent as skirts and dresses were never worn without one. The "sharkskin" variety were very pretty and although comfortable to wear, as well as sorting out the static problem, the stiffness of the material didn't do a lot for the lines of some of the clothes which slid over the material sometimes, causing them to ride up. It wasn't until the late 1960s that the first fabric conditioners solved that problem as well as seeing the last of the underskirt for everyday wear.

As with skirt lengths, women's trouser widths have never really been one style or another since the 60s, although the high waist has disappeared for the most part.

At the age of twelve to thirteen, girls reached a milestone as they graduated from ankle socks to wearing nylons held up by suspender belts. Julie treated Monica to her first pair of nylons and suspender belt which coincided with mum buying her her first mini dress. Looking back now, Monica says she rode her bike round the roads of Kirkby, aged thirteen, wearing a green empire line short dress, with her suspender belt in full view of all those she passed, in all innocence.

Before I left school, fashion was just something I dreamt about. A black polo neck sweater worn with a pair of slacks was one of the latest trends and something I longed for, when I was fourteen. I discussed this with my school friends, saying I was going to ask could I have them for Christmas, knowing full well that I had no chance. Another of dad's rules was that girls didn't wear trousers and I was only able to have my first pair after I had left school. Julie went regularly to the Silver Blades ice rink in Kensington with her friends, for which she wore slacks. She took me with her just the once when I was ten. I loved the experience even though I did more falling than skating but I didn't get hurt wearing the outgrown pair of slacks Julie had given me to wear. She told me I could keep them afterwards so I put them on the following day and was a bit stunned when dad told me to take them off. He said girls didn't wear trousers. No amount of protesting from me or Julie could change his mind. There was never any getting round dad if he closed his mind.

My older brothers hadn't really been involved in the earlier fashions of winklepickers and drainpipe trousers, much as they may have liked to. Eddie said instead of drainpipes, he wore the 24 inch bottoms handed down from dad, with a turn up sewn by mum, completed by the black leather shoes he proudly polished, stuffed with cardboard to fill the holes.

The boys did follow the hair styles with the help of Brylcreem to style and to keep their hair in place. I once read somewhere that by applying a minute amount of Brylcreem to your hair, it acted to de-frizz hair tending to curl, especially in the damp weather. I tried this one night before I went to bed, while still at school, carefully applying the smallest amount. When I woke up the following morning my hair was a mass of grease and I was left with no choice but to go to school as it was, plastered to my head. I spent the day denying that I was wearing nit ointment. I'm not sure what happened to Brylcreem when the boys started to grow their hair long but the majority of them seemed to take pride in their silky, grease free locks.

The 1960s brought their own ever changing women's hairstyles. Rollers, previously worn overnight, were removed for the last time as we started to blow dry our hair, releasing so many women from hairstyles previously doomed by frizz. Efforts to straighten or smooth hair up until then had involved sleeping all night in rollers held in place with giant sized clips sticking into your scalp; occasional ironing of hair, or to tame a wavy fringe, sleeping with sellotape on your forehead. The bouffant styles which had involved back combing, gave way to the sleek styles made possible by the addition of the nozzle on hair dryers which really did transform the lives of some women, giving them more choice in how they wore their "crowning glory". Hair tending to frizz, especially in damp weather, could now be made sleek and shiny and the more coarse, frizzy hair types could be transformed to glossy curls, all without the need for rollers. The midi hair style which came into fashion was perfect for anybody with hair like mine that tended to wave. The hair was cut to sit on the shoulders, then layered from the nape of the neck up. The beauty of this style was the versatility as it suited curly or straight hair and I found it very easy to manage.

Since I was eleven, travelling to school on the No 92 bus, I had sat beside the women going to work at Jacobs biscuit factory on Long Lane in Fazakerley, with their hair in rollers underneath a headscarf, tied at the chin. This fascinated me as I wondered how it must feel not to worry that you were having what we now call a bad hair day. The rollers gradually gave way to sleek hairstyles as the women left their curlers behind in favour of the new styles.

Hair curlers have never completely disappeared and running parallel with the blow dryer we also had heated rollers such as the Carmen brand which I found to be a big improvement on ordinary rollers. Mine came with conditioning lotion which removed all traces of frizz. I simply got up in the morning, plugged the set in, made a cup of tea, drinking it as I put the rollers in my hair, got washed and dressed for work, before taking the curlers out and combing my hair before I walked out of the door.

The best hairdryer I have ever had was made by

Ronson in the late 1960s. This again, suited my hair well. In fact it was perfect, being versatile enough to be used for most hair types and styles. While it looked big and cumbersome, it was surprisingly easy to use. The motor was housed in a circular case and it had a hose of about three feet long, similar to a vacuum cleaner hose, with the styling brush attached to the end.

The hair care products of the day were limited to shampoo, setting lotion and hair lacquer. I never used the setting lotion myself but often watched the hairdressers using it to set the curls while doing a shampoo and set. I remember it as a heavily scented, pale blue liquid which came in small, clear bottles. The only type of conditioner on the market was a "creme rinse" which we would buy as an occasional treat from the top shop, to soften the hair and leave a lovely shine. Some of the women of mum's generation left all of their hair care to the hairdressers, calling in once a week for their shampoo and set, and indeed this practice still prevails today for some ladies, of course. The rest of us washed our hair usually twice a week, not nearly as often as today, but then we didn't have facilities of today like showers, or even bathrooms in some houses.

There were some excellent hair colour rinses around at that time, such as Harmony, packaged in a triangular shaped little box. It worked by simply washing in, leaving for twenty minutes before washing out and would last through several washes. The rinse also acted as a very good conditioner which combined with the colour, left the hair lustrous and glossy. Another product on the market, used by blondes and brunettes alike, was Hiltone. As well as lightening dark blonde hair it could turn mousy coloured hair blonde and turn brunettes a shade lighter. I loved Hiltone from the first time I tried it myself, when I uncovered a lovely shade of chestnut which looked very natural. I hit upon a problem when the roots started to show through as it was tricky to apply the lotion to the new growth, without creating multi coloured tones, so whenever the darker roots started to show through too much I would apply a darker rinse to return to my natural colour. When I called into a chemist shop on the way home from work one night to buy such a rinse, the assistant looked at my hair and asked why I wanted to change such a beautiful colour so I muttered something about not liking it, pleased that it looked natural but disappointed because it had to go, for a while anyway. I didn't know of anybody who paid a hairdresser to colour their hair - it was all done at home as far as I was aware, resulting in a lot of straw coloured hair to be seen.

During the mid to late 1960s, a heavy scent fell over most of Britain, by courtesy of Youth Dew, the perfume by Estée Lauder, as any woman who was anybody, had to have a bottle. The perfume itself was very oily, very strong and very expensive. I not only loved the smell but also how it lingered on your clothes afterwards, obliterating the smell of cigarettes, or so I thought. By the time Youth Dew did go out of fashion it had seen the launch of the Estée Lauder empire which of course still continues to flourish. My own particular favourite perfumes of the era were Apple Blossom by Helena Rubenstein, as I have previously said, then next came Worth by Je Revien which is still on the shelves today. I sometimes catch the scent of Youth Dew, and looking round I will spot an elderly, always glamorous looking lady, and wonder if she has used the perfume through the decades. I have been tempted by the Worth bottles on the perfume shelves but have not succumbed yet as it would feel like going into a time warp to wear it now. It could be that I'm too young to wear it just now.

Many of the brand names of cosmetics on the market during the 1960s are still here today with the products having been modified over the years to suit the changes in trends. During the 60s, pastel shades in lipstick took the place of the deeper reds, giving a softer look. Generally, the foundations and face powders were fairly heavy and obvious and didn't achieve the more natural look of today, especially when pan stick or thick, creamy foundations were used as a base, to be set with heavy powder. Again, we had Twiggy as our role model with the emphasis being very much on the eyes. There were varying shades of blue and green eyeshadows which were coordinated with pale creamy colours with white around the outer eye area as a highlighter.

While I was still at school Julie had an eyeshadow in Midnight Blue which I would experiment with in the bathroom mirror. Whenever I did this, I would always be caught out one way or the other by mum either knocking on the bathroom door or calling up to me to help her. I then had to scrub away at my face to get the stuff off. I used to love the experimenting. I would start by seeing what the make up looked like when applied properly then get carried away and paint it on as thick as I could. I would then swear innocence when Julie wondered what had happened to her make up.

Eye liner was the pièce de résistance in the make up process. Applied by firstly pencilling over and under the outer eyelids, we then drew a dark line marking out the eye socket. The lid was then filled in with a dark shade of shadow, to achieve the panda look of Dusty Springfield, although this would be modified during the day.

Mascara hasn't changed much from the little tubes we have now with the wand, apart from the type that came in a small palette with a separate brush that had to be licked, before being dipped into a solid block of mascara in a tray. I never used it myself but was once intrigued as I watched a friend using it, wondering why she bothered. She said she liked it because the amount you could load on was limitless.

Twiggy set the trend for false eyelashes for evening wear but I found them too messy to apply and to keep on. They were like thick, plastic spiders covered in glue. I was practising putting some on one night at the mirror over the fireplace in the front room when dad walked in to speak to me. I had one lash on and tried not to blink while talking to him but fortunately he didn't notice.

Cassie, our Avon Lady did well out of us girls, calling at the house once a fortnight. She lived in one of the new private houses built on Kirkby Row and supplemented the family income by selling Avon. The brand may not have been the cutting edge in cosmetics but there was something to suit everybody and the beauty of buying that way was that you could test anything you ordered from Cassie's stock as well as receiving free samples to test for her next visit. Again, the perfumes were not the top brands and I heard it said that Avon perfume all smelled the same, but I liked the fact that they were light and fresh in contrast to the more expensive, heavier brands. It was never an Avon brand of makeup that we would discard into a drawer, having found it wasn't suitable.

Before the days of sunbeds, the rest of our skin would remain much as God had made it, which was very pale in my case as I didn't tan very well. There were fake tan products available to experiment with, which I tried myself once.

As with some of today's fake tans, the lotion worked overnight and I applied it liberally before going to bed one night, covering my arms, neck, shoulders and my face as I wanted to make sure all that was visible had an even colour. I woke up the following morning to a sickly smell and a mahogany coloured face, neck and arms. This was during the summertime and I caught the train to work, wearing a white dress with a lemony coloured bodice, which set off my "tan" well. I was very conscious of the contrast between my usual complexion but as there wasn't much I could do about it, I made the most of having a nice tan, if a bit overdone.

I had a seat on the train that morning on the way to work, with one of my travelling companions and as we sat on the full train, she commented on my tan, asking me in front of everyone where I had been. It was an awkward situation as I would have happily told her it was a fake tan but didn't want to announce it to the rest of the passengers, who we were facing, so I said I had sat in the back garden all day Sunday. She looked a bit concerned as she told me to be careful not to burn myself, while I sat there wondering how anybody could be so daft as to think it was real.

On the return journey home that day my skin resembled a peeling new potato, with the remainder of the colour being washed off in the bath later on. I went to work the following day a whiter shade of pale, with my arms covered up to avoid attention and if anybody noticed then they never said.

We tried more natural methods of getting a tan, such as daubing ourselves in olive oil and vinegar then sitting in the garden for hours, to come back indoors more or less the same colour. Sun factors were introduced around this time and Monica tells me how on a weekend trip to Blackpool with mum and dad, along with Sheila, they misunderstood the purpose of the cream, thinking it was intended to produce a tan, daubed themselves in it and wondered why it hadn't worked.

So where did we head to when all dressed to impress? While the boys mostly stayed in Kirkby, playing snooker at the Kirkby Tenants Club or the Connie Club, the girls made their debut at the Grafton Ballroom on West Derby Road, from the age of around sixteen. Then when we were a bit older and were ready to graduate from half a pint of cider, we went to the clubs and pubs in Liverpool town. We hadn't been educated in alcohol at home as mum and dad didn't drink apart from the Christmas sherry or occasional bottle of liqueur on special occasions, and they didn't go to pubs. In fact come to think of it, I don't ever remember seeing a bottle of wine in our house. We therefore went by example and on my first visit to a pub I watched to see what other people were drinking. When I heard a girl ask for a lager and lime, that was what I ordered. This progressed to Babycham, followed by the ruby red, sweet tasting and very potent Cherry B, both of which came in third pint bottles. As a fully fledged drinker, barley wine or whisky and lime were to become my usual although I do remember drinking Guinness for some time but can't remember how or when that started but I do remember struggling at first to swallow the drink before I acquired the taste. I must have been quite healthy at that time with all that iron I was taking in.

If the term "binge drinker" means going out and drinking yourself senseless then that is what I eventually became, at weekends, when I didn't have to be up for work the next morning. As far as I was concerned it was just a part of growing up and lots of us did it. Not that I would advocate anybody to drink to excess, I'm just telling it as it was.

I'll just touch on the subject of drugs at this point. Margaret once said to me how lucky we were that we didn't get involved with drugs during the 60s, as some of the people we mixed with, including one very close friend of mine, did. We could have easily taken a wrong turn but well, fortunately something stopped us and we were never persuaded.

I would often meet up after work with Ann, my friend from school, while she was working in the accounts department at George Henry Lee. When we were invited to join some of the store managers for a drink one evening we accepted happily. Sitting in a pub on Hanover Street, we hadn't eaten since lunch time and the drink went to our heads so much so that when we both went to the ladies at the same time, we couldn't leave again as we were both unable to stand up, let alone walk out of the room. One of the barmaids was eventually sent in to check on us and when she found us both slumped against the walls, she told us she had just the thing for us. She returned a few minutes later with two small glasses containing a dark brown liquid which she called "Corpse Reviver". Ann and I had never heard of it before but both gladly accepted the drinks which I learnt afterwards were a brandy based concoction. Whatever was in the drinks, they certainly worked, very quickly, as no sooner had we finishing drinking than we were able to stand up fairly straight and walk out of the ladies room, feeling a bit embarrassed.

I never saw a girl drink from a pint glass in the 60s as it wasn't the done thing. We had our own, more delicate half pint glasses, known to some people of Liverpool as "a tart's glass". Although calling somebody a "tart" was a derogatory term generally used as a sleight on a girl's virtue, the word "tart" was an inoffensive name for a woman in Liverpool at the time. During one of Monica's student jobs working as a barmaid in the Pes Espada club in Liverpool, boyfriends and husbands, ever conscious of being seen to be the perfect gentlemen and in an effort to ensure their partner was treated with respect, would remind the bar staff to, "Serve hers in a tart's glass."

Burgers were always a favourite once the pubs turned out until late in the 60s when bar meals became popular, especially in the quieter, out of town pubs. As chickens became more readily available for everyday meals, "chicken in the basket", served with chips, could be the highlight of a night out as it was still something considered to be reserved for special occasions.

Meeting boyfriends and girlfriends was a bit more formal than today as to round a night off you were quite likely to be invited to go for a "meal" at the end of a night out, from somebody you had just met. This would be a proper sit down, knife and fork affair, possibly in the night club you were already in. I disliked that idea and would always refuse as it wasn't my idea of relaxation. I would definitely much prefer the kebab culture of today.

Chapter Thirteen

The Visit

In our ever expanding family there is always some celebration or other on the horizon as indeed was the case on the day of the recent christening of John's two little granddaughters, held in south Liverpool. I travelled with Eddie and his wife, Pat, driving through Aughton on our way to the church. Whenever I travel out that way with Eddie, we take the opportunity to drive around remembering the names and places from the past.

On the way home later, Eddie pulled in at The Chesterfield, the pub which replaced St Mary's school. We knew the restaurant had closed some time ago and there was a For Sale board outside the restaurant. It was very quiet and we couldn't see anybody around but two cars were parked outside the house within the grounds so as Eddie parked up alongside the building and we got out of the car to have a look round, we were careful not to intrude as we watched out for signs of life at the house. We looked, as best we could, into a brick built, rendered building, about 12 ft wide x 5 ft high, which housed what looked like an oil tank. This was just next to the main building and as we tried to get a perspective of the siting of the old school, I said to Eddie that the building that housed the oil tank looked very much like "the places" building to me. We had to climb up a bit of an incline and squeeze through bushes to get a better look over the top of the brick building as it didn't have a roof, where we could just about make out the pipes leading to the tank. The only way I could get down the little hill was to run as there was nothing to hold on to. I had fallen and broken my wrist a couple of weeks earlier and was wearing a cast but as I ran down that hill, all the fears of falling I'd had since breaking my wrist were temporarily forgotten.

We left for home, saying we would come back soon to have a better look. I spoke to Monica later and the three of us arranged to go back during the following week. No-one else could make it and we didn't want to put it off so it was all arranged for the following Thursday. It happened that it would have been dad's birthday on this particular day and when one of us mentioned it during our visit, it became clear that we had all had dad's birthday in mind as we walked round.

Thursday turned out to be a lovely August day, one of the very few we had all summer when it didn't rain and the sun shined. We met up with Monica at the school. I had contacted the property agents and been told that an offer had been made on the restaurant which included the house and as both the restaurant and the house were unoccupied, we could have a better look round without disturbing anybody.

The first thing we went to see was the old well which we could see was the original, as the chamber was only partly concealed by a couple of concrete slabs. It has been made into a feature now, with a more traditional looking cover over it, rather than the hole in the ground we had to beware of at school.

Most of the windows of the main building were open, which was surprising as there were snooker cues lying around and empty beer glasses, all clearly visible to an opportunist thief. Eddie said it looked as though there had recently been a private party and people had just walked out without clearing away. He could be right and it could be that private functions were still being held.

The places

We looked closely at the structure of the main building and could see that most of it was in fact from the original school which didn't seem to have been demolished as we had thought, having been redeveloped instead. What was more surprising was that looking at the shape of the building, it appeared to have been extended to incorporate the old air raid shelter which was now the back wall. This was all of course nostalgic to us and we were pleased to see that the school building had been preserved. We had another look at the oil tank building and it is definitely "the places".

I took a couple of snaps to refresh my memory, intending to come back another time to get better pictures. Monica told me I must include one of Bride's garage which is still next to the school grounds and where John spent his last afternoon at St Mary's, removing graffiti from the garage window. I took the picture of the building which looks exactly the same now as it did all those years ago. Of course I couldn't recapture John at work on the window but if I close my eyes I can imagine the caricatures of the teachers and the few choice words he was writing, using paint left outside by the garage owner. John would be tall and skinny with a short back and sides haircut. He would be wearing knee length grey flannel trousers held up with braces, half mast knee length grey socks with black lace up shoes, round blue National Health glasses - and a grin.

Bride's garage

We then drove down to St Kentigern's church for another look round. It was sad but not surprising to see several broken windows, as nothing much is sacred these days, not even a church. As we were leaving, Eddie picked up a piece of the bough of a tree and handed it to me, telling me to keep it as a memento. The wood was sopping wet and smelled of rot and I looked at it dubiously at first but then took it happily saying I would dry it out and maybe varnish it, or do something to get rid of the smell. The wood has now been daubed in layers of varnish and still smells musty but I keep it in a drawer in my kitchen.

As I was stretching up to look through the church windows at one point I heard Monica telling Eddie I'd be looking for ghosts so I said, "If ever I'm going to find one, it'll be today!" I had a feeling which I didn't fully understand, that the day was special in some way.

We left the church and drove down to The Horse and Jockey pub just down the road. Eddie had suggested going to the pub for lunch but I had brought a picnic as it was such a lovely day so we decided to walk down to the canal, a bit further along, to have our lunch, intending to return to the pub for a drink.

The well trodden footpaths and the murky waters of the Leeds and Liverpool canal hold 300 years worth of memories of the work involved in carrying goods from city to city. The waters will bear witness to life's secrets and dramas as they unfolded, hidden from the houses just a few hundred yards away. The canal also will still offer a haven to the fishermen dotted along the banks, sitting in silence. Eddie's tiny role, on our bit of the canal, was to fish with his brothers and friends, up until the time he married and left Kirkby, and he chatted away about his memories as we walked along. The boys always said how no talking was allowed while they were fishing as it disturbed the fish and I could never understand the pleasure to be had from sitting in silence, from the crack of dawn, often cold and wet, on the off chance of catching a decent sized or type of fish, to be looked at before being thrown back into the water. Thinking back now, I am surprised Eddie could keep quiet for long but thinking again, he is actually quite deep and perhaps that was part of the attraction of going fishing, the sanctuary of a quiet place. Actually thinking about it more, it doesn't sound such a bad idea and perhaps more of us should try it. Eddie still fishes with his sons.

As we walked along, he reminded us of the coal merchants who supplied our coal from their premises down by the canal bank. During the very severe winter of 1958, he was sent with Gerry when they were aged 11 and 13, to have the pram filled up with coal at a cost of 1/6d (eight new pence) as we were getting through more coal than usual and had run out between deliveries. It would have taken the boys about an hour and a half to make the round trip, trudging through the snow. The coal merchant's young daughter served them with the coal for which they handed over the money. Mum gave the boys the money to pay as she knew the coal merchant's rule was strictly cash payments on delivery or collection and they would never give coal out that wasn't paid for. Their children were also well aware of the rules. When the delivery man next called he knocked on the door to be paid, including the 1/6d for the pram full of coal the boys had collected, insisting that it hadn't been paid for and mum had to pay again or not get any coal. There's no way the boys wouldn't have paid on the day, after making their way to collect the coal, apart from the fact that they wouldn't have been so dishonest, because they wouldn't have run any risk of hanging round in the cold and pushing an empty pram home, to face mum. I think Eddie still feels hurt by what happened and I can't blame him, he's as honest as can be.

We noted the chip shop still in exactly the same spot as it always was, and a few other places either changed or unchanged, before arriving at the canal bank. We were getting a bit pushed for time and didn't have to walk very far before we came to a grassy patch which was ideal for sitting down, so Monica and I did so. Eddie remained on his feet, pacing around, and as he was eating his sandwiches and chatting away, he leaned over and started scratching at a small gravelled area and said, "Look what I've found."

I thought, "Here we go, he hasn't changed, he's found 20p." But it wasn't 20p that he handed me. It wasn't a coin. It was a small gold cross.

Chapter Fourteen

Holidays

I love boats and I love water, and looking out over the Irish Sea, I'm trying to imagine what it must be like to have boarded an ocean liner. I've seen films where people emigrate to America where the landing stages are crowded with crying people waving their families off, sometimes forever. I can't think of anything much worse than knowing you'll never see your family again, apart from dying.

I wonder how Auntie May felt when she went to live abroad. Maybe she always intended to come back as indeed she did, but that meant Uncle Joe left his family behind. One of the girls in our class emigrated to Australia last year. Apparently the passage only cost £10 for each member of the family and her mum and dad said the life out there is so much better and easier than here. I'm not sure what they meant by that or what's so bad here that they wanted to get away from. Maybe it's the sunshine and beaches that are the attraction - like being on one long holiday.

I will travel when I'm older but I will always come back. I want to visit Malaya where Leha lives and to go to Singapore where mum's brother, Uncle Eddie spent time during the war. He's a pilot in the RAF who married a Scottish lady and lives up in Scotland now so we never see him. I would also like to go to Russia to see how the people live, and I would like to see New York.

There were no crowds to wave us off today from the Pier Head as we alighted the "Manx Maid" on our way to the Isle of Man for two weeks.

My reflections are interrupted by Julie calling me. She's asking me to round the little ones up. The last time I saw them they were playing downstairs on the car turntable so I wouldn't be surprised if one of them had been sick by now. It seems the ticket inspector is asking dad to identify whoever is with him to check we all have a ticket as he's seen a load of children running round. It was time to move away from the edge of the boat anyway because it's getting a bit cold and I'm shivering.

This must be the fifth or six time I have been to the Isle of Man and although mum and dad like Kirk Michael more than anywhere else on the island and we stay there most years, we have never stayed in the same cottage twice. Each year when the owner of the holiday home opens the door to all ten of us standing there I think they get a bit of a shock, thinking they have the orphanage on their doorstep and although they seem reassured once they have had a chat with mum and dad, they do tend to lurk around and knock at the door at regular intervals, trying to look inside. I suppose you can't really blame them but when mum told us that it is often their own homes they have let out while they stay with relatives during the holiday season, I can't help thinking they can't expect to have their cake and eat it. If they leave all their nice things in their own home for other people to use then the chances are there will be some damage done. We've never done any damage inside a house so far but they aren't all full of valuables - some are pretty sparsely equipped and mum always stashes away anything of value.

We've arrived at the cottage and have been through the preliminaries with the owner, a Mrs Cannell, who chatted smilingly throughout, seemingly undaunted by the room full of us fidgeting and all talking at the same time, straining to explore upstairs to claim our beds............

We're upstairs now and although the cottage is quite small, there are three sets of bunk beds in two rooms as well as mum and dad's room, so we'll fit in fine, although the top bunk that John has just been bouncing on didn't seem all that sturdy. There's a huge, overgrown garden at the back of the cottage with lots of goosegog bushes which Mrs Cannell very kindly told mum to help herself to, suggesting we take a bowl each to fill. I like this lady - she seems very understanding and kind.

The kitchen and living room are fair sized and when I peeped through the door to a tiny sitting room while mum and dad were being shown round, I saw a lovely dark wooden Welsh dresser, like I've seen in photographs and on television, chock-a-block with china. I'll have to investigate the room the first chance I get as mum told us the minute Mrs Cannell's back was turned that the room is out of bounds, but surely no harm will be done if I go in on my own. Then again I had better not actually pick the china up. I saw a piano as well! We could have such fun with that if only mum and dad would let us..........

I'm in the sitting room now as mum and dad have gone for a walk in Glen Wyllin which I think is mum's favourite place in the world and I can understand why. The gardens have the most beautiful flowers and the whole glen is surrounded by rose bushes. Next to playing on a beach, seeing the flowers is the best part of a holiday for me. They are everywhere.

That particular holiday was memorable for two reasons. Firstly, for the gooseberry pies we had after tea every night of the holiday. The other highlight was that it was during another of mum and dad's walks in Glen Wyllin that I had my first driving lesson, from John, aged ten. He had obviously been itching to get hold of the car keys because he picked them up as soon as mum and dad left the house and when I asked him what he was up to he asked me if I would like to learn to drive. That didn't seem like a bad idea so I happily jumped into the car, ready for my lesson, aged thirteen. All was going well as I was taken through the gears, over and over again and I can remember being overawed as I tried to digest it all, wondering how to remember everything. We hit upon a problem as the car was parked on a bit of a hill on a narrow driveway which sloped down at the edges and suddenly the car started to roll backwards. John hadn't said anything about reversing; he obviously hadn't watched dad doing that bit closely enough. I screamed out as the car began to roll down the hill and to the side of the driveway but John managed to stop it. He can't have been as scared as I was because he wanted to drive back to where we started from so dad wouldn't know the car had been moved. I had to insist he got out with me to face the music with dad which was surely preferable to being dead.

We didn't get to play the piano.

With the Isle of Man being such a small island, only about 32 miles wide by less than half that distance in length, we covered a lot of it on foot when the weather was fine or, in later years, when dad took the car, we could drive round the whole island to visit the ports. Port Erin was always our favourite beach and we also visited Port St Mary once or twice but it wasn't as nice. We only ever went to Castletown once as apart from the castle, compared with the rest of the island it seemed a bit bleak.

Douglas, the island's capital was the place for the high life on the Island. We never spent much time there as children but did have a walk round one day while waiting to catch the ferry home, after dad had parked his blue Ford Anglia along the prom. While we were walking round Monica complained of not feeling very well so mum told her to go back to the car to wait for us. When we returned to find the car empty we were all frantic as we ran in all directions looking for Monica who was eventually found safe and well, a five minute walk away, wondering what all the fuss was about as she sat, reading, in the back seat of an identical car. That provided our entertainment for the trip home as we laughed all the way.

I returned to the Isle of Man just the once when I was older, after dad had died, with Mum, Margaret, Monica and Sheila. We stayed in Douglas for a long weekend, where the majority of our time was spent at the Summerland entertainment centre which the British Tourist Authority claimed was unequalled throughout the world. It was a huge complex of over a square mile in size with entertainment to suit everybody and we particularly liked the roller skating rink which we visited every day. One single tune was played constantly at the centre. It was "I'm forever blowing bubbles", which did grate on the nerves as time went by.

I can remember the building always feeling too hot and not very comfortable and I would take time out of the skating rink to sit just outside the room at the bottom of the stairs to take a bit of air from the main entrance. While sitting on the stairs one afternoon I was approached by a security guard who pointed out that it wasn't safe to sit on the stairs, as if ever there was a fire then there would be a stampede down the stairs. That much was obvious when I thought about it and realised how true it was. When I heard, just two years later that Summerland had been completely destroyed by fire, the security man's words were ringing in my ears.

During that visit, Monica, Margaret and I decided to hire bikes, thinking it would be a good idea to visit the TT race track. We asked the attendant at the bike hire shop if he could point us in the right direction. He was somehow under the misapprehension that we wanted to ride round the whole of the track as he proceeded to give us detailed directions. We couldn't look at each other as the minutes went by with him outlining the route of the track, with great enthusiasm, but we did manage to hold it together until he asked us how long we wanted to hire the bikes for, asking would one day be enough as it was quite a trek we were planning. It was then that we looked at each other as we almost collapsed with laughter, after telling the poor man that the minimum one hour's hire would be quite sufficient.

My childhood love of bikes was just a memory at this stage as I hadn't ridden for a few years and while it is true that you never forget how to ride a bike, you can lose your nerve, as I was to find out. I didn't have any problem riding round the quiet country roads but when I found myself careering down a steep, hilly road leading to the centre of Peel, that's when I realised how out of practice I was. I could see Monica and Margaret riding ahead of me, in complete control, but I wasn't. I was terrified, sitting with my feet off the pedals, free wheeling with my legs outstretched, not knowing how to control the bike. I did somehow manage to stop, or to be more precise, fall off, slap bang in the centre of traffic, under the watchful eye of a policeman who asked me if they didn't they have such things as traffic lights where I came from. Monica and Margaret were the ones who had trouble staying on their bikes on the return journey as they seemed to have found it funny.

I didn't know much about what the boys got up to half the time when we were children so when I first told Eddie I was putting this story together and he smiled and said, "We were swines", that wasn't quite the reaction I expected so I told him that he was missing the point. He smiled again as he said quietly, "No, we were swines."

Then when I first spoke to John, he didn't have much to say for a minute or so then he too smiled and said quietly, "I was a horrible child". I told him that wasn't true and not to be harsh on himself but he laughed and said, "No, I was a horrible child." He turned to Christine, his wife since they were both just turned eighteen and said, "I hope that won't put you off love." Christine said, "No, your mum told me you were a horrible child so I knew that when I married you."

I know a fair bit more now of the things they got up to as boys and it's been a learning curve after which I might just have to concede that perhaps I should agree with them.

Talking to Gerry about our Isle of Man holidays he asked me did I remember the place we stayed at in Kirk Michael that had an orchard when we first arrived. I do remember there being barely a leaf left on a tree at one cottage we stayed in by the time we went home, let alone any fruit. Apparently, when mum sent him and Eddie to the bakers in the village each morning, they would skim up the trees to raid the orchard on the way, to throw apples at the cows, and no doubt the occasional bull if one happened to be around.

It wasn't always the Isle of Man where we went on holiday. We paid a few visits to the Lake District in later years. Julie and John, who was still her boyfriend at that time, helped transport us to and from Kendal one year. Margaret and I travelled with mum and dad on the way home after the week's visit. We watched and listened in horror, when dad missed his turn off on the motorway so he quickly did a U turn and drove the few miles back, driving in the wrong direction. I couldn't believe what he was doing as I watched the expression on his face, defying anyone to notice. One helpful motorist passed us, waving and beeping as he went by, and dad wound the window down to shout, "I know I am you stupid bugger". Dad prided himself on never having had an accident, which was true, and according to him, the roads were full of idiots.

The one time we went to Anglesey would have lived on in the memories of the residents for a long time and who knows, they could have dined out on stories of our visit for years. I've never been back to Anglesey and although I've been to Wales many times since, I never quite fancied a return visit there.

The Anglesey house, from memory, was a huge, grey building in the middle of nowhere with nothing to do apart from going to the beach. There were no other holidaymakers in the vicinity so nobody to make friends with, so whenever we weren't at the beach we had to amuse ourselves as best we could.

The owner of the house was a Mr Taylor, a dour faced man if ever I saw one, who spent the whole of the two weeks hanging round, watching every move we made. The house, which was dark inside, with wood panelled walls throughout, was partly out of bounds to us because mum wasn't taking any chances with what she called, "The miserable old so-and-so's old rubbish that he seems to care so much about." The house was a long walk from the beach and we would be accompanied by mum and dad on most days but being on holiday didn't stop the work for them. There was always food to prepare, cleaning and washing etc. and on the days we didn't venture far we would spend most of our time amusing ourselves around the area of the house. In fact the best entertainment for the girls was a very wide, white painted wooden gate at the bottom of the long driveway to the house. We spent many a happy hour swinging on the gate until Mr Taylor complained to dad that we might damage it and asked us to stop. As things turned out he would have been better keeping his eye on the boys instead of worrying about a few little girls damaging his gate.

The boys had gone off exploring, as was to be expected, they were on holiday after all and it was quite natural and healthy for them to be outdoors. It turned out that they had found a treasure in the form of an old cast iron bath they'd come across lying at the edge of a field. The bath was near to a small body of water which, according to Eddie was about 15/20 square feet in size. There followed an afternoon of joy, spent pushing the dirty old bath towards the water. I don't know what they thought they would do with a cast iron bath because it could hardly be used as a boat but in the event, it became lodged at the edge of the lake and they abandoned any ideas they did have and spent a happy hour throwing stones into the "boat" surrounding the water instead.

A man out walking his dog passed by and stopped to watch them throwing the stones. He didn't say anything to the lads but went on his way and they thought nothing of it until he returned ten minutes later with three other men in tow, headed by Mr Taylor whose face seemed to have turned purple. It didn't take long for the boys to sense trouble so they scarpered with Mr Taylor's posse giving full chase. The boys waited for the dust to settle before returning to the house but when they did get back they found a reception committee waiting for them. Poor mum and dad were being threatened with the authorities having been told that the boys had contaminated the local water supply. We were half way through the second week of our holiday at this time and mum and dad were made to feel very uncomfortable for the rest of our stay. Then when Gerry's rickety old bed collapsed beneath him the day before we were due to leave, mum and dad decided they'd had enough and we left for home a day early.

We returned to Wales but to a different town the next time.

We were bouncing around with excitement on that Saturday morning as the holiday was only booked on the last minute as we didn't know until the Friday night whether mum and dad could find somewhere affordable. Dad found out from somebody at work about this place called Talacre and he managed to hire a bungalow, purported to be close to Talacre beach, for two weeks. Dad's trusty Hillman Imp accommodated mum and dad and four out of the remaining eight of us. A plan was hatched which was very efficient in theory but which unfortunately didn't quite work. The plan was for Mum and dad to travel to Wales on a first shift, then dad would do a quick turn around and drive out to Chester railway station where the rest of us would meet him, having caught the train from Kirkby. Julie was in charge of Gerry, Eddie and me, as we made our way to Chester which was all a bit of an adventure. Things started to go wrong when our connecting train to take us to Chester was cancelled and we were about an hour late arriving. When we eventually arrived, dad, who had been waiting all that time, was anxious to get back to Talacre as he said he wasn't too happy at what he had seen there.

We arrived to find mum upset and dad had a proper chance to look around as the "bungalow" they had booked was nothing more than a wooden shed with the "rooms" partitioned by curtains. The holiday site was isolated from civilisation, there were no shops in the vicinity and the beach was a long hike away, rather than the easy walking distance that dad had been given to understand. After a heated discussion dad had with the owner, we returned home, having to repeat the same staggered performance as before. What a let down that turned out to be. The journey home was miserable and I can still remember walking into the house feeling dejected but the one highlight of the trip was the fish and chip shop we managed to find on the way home.

As we got older, gradually, we dropped off going away with mum and dad then after Julie was married, Gerry, Eddie, Margaret and I stayed at home while they went away with the younger ones. Dad had a motorbike at the time to use for travelling to and from work and although he had let Gerry have a go while under his supervision, he left strict instructions that he was not to go anywhere near the bike while they were away. This caution was completely ignored and despite protests from the rest of us, Gerry rode off one Saturday afternoon on the bike dad had cleaned and polished until it shone. He returned hours later after no doubt impressing his friends on a dirt track in Melling, used by the lads who owned their own motorbikes. The bike was filthy and Gerry's half hearted attempts to clean it up didn't impress dad when he came home when there was hell to pay.

We had a lot of fun on those holidays where the boys' antics were nothing more than a mixture of high spirits, mischief and brainlessness. I personally lived the whole year looking forward to going away so much.

Whichever way we spent those times away, it wasn't

all parents who managed to take a family such as the size of ours on a summer holiday each year, and I'm sure they didn't see it this way, but mum and dad should have been proud of themselves.

The house in Anglesey

Monica and John in Kirk Michael

Chapter Fifteen

Christmas

It's three o'clock on Boxing Day morning - the middle of the night. Dad lit a fire in our room again last night and as I stirred in my sleep I caught sight of the glow from the dying embers in the grate. I lay staring into the fireplace for a while, warm and comfortable in the absolute cosiness of it all but now, as this will be the last time for a long time that I will see the fire burn, and even though outside the bed covers it is freezing cold, I'm now sitting up, wrapped in my eiderdown, watching the occasional flicker from the grate cast shadows around the room, as I reflect on Christmas and the past couple of weeks, as my sisters sleep.

I'm looking back to just over two weeks ago, to the Saturday afternoon, when I stood in the bay window with Margaret, John, Monica and Sheila to wave mum and dad off on a shopping trip to town...............

It was snowing last time we looked out but lifting the nets to wipe the condensation from the windows, we can see that it's beginning to turn to sleet already and the earlier snowfall is fast turning to slush. I wouldn't have minded but mum asked me and Margaret to mind the little ones while they are out and we had hoped we would be able to play in the snow. Any thoughts of making a snowman are quickly abandoned at the thought of icy cold sleet dripping down my neck. I shudder at the thought of it as I turn from the window to survey the front room which can only be described as an unholy tip, as I decide what to do next. The place is such a mess - after the morning's activities of dad bringing the Christmas tree and decorations down from the loft. The said tree is standing looking dejected, propped up in the corner of the room alongside four battered looking cardboard boxes overflowing with multi coloured strands of tissue paper and tinsel, trailing to the floor with slivers of paper all through the hall and this floor.

Poor dad, we'd been asking him for days to get the tree down and Margaret met him at the door as he came in last night, before he'd had a chance to take his coat off, asking him about the decorations. He said if he hears anyone else ask, "What about the decorations, dad?" then there won't bloodywell be any. Well, they're down now so we're ok although looking through the boxes it looked like half the stuff needed ditching so we've decided to go to the town centre to buy some crepe paper to make new garlands. Another check out of the window shows that nothing is falling from the sky at the moment and at least we will keep warm by walking..............

We've been back an hour now, having been to Woolworths to stock up with multi coloured sheets of paper. I've just managed to get John in from the back garden. He found bits of snow which had drifted into corners of the garden so in the end I said he could have ten minutes to play because we stood for that long at the back door asking him to come in that all the heat from the fire was escaping. Before I knew it the garden was full of his mates so I gave up and let them play. He now looks like a drowned rat so we'd better make sure he's dried off before he gets pneumonia and before mum sees him, or I'll be in trouble...............

In the meantime we finished the garlands and threw the left over bits of paper on the fire then we all gave the place a good tidy and polish as a surprise for mum to save her a midnight job...............

We've now had our tea and are all trying to help dad put the decorations up. He's moving the hall table round to stand on to reach up to put the drawing pins in the ceilings and he nearly fell off just now as we were all bumping into each other until somebody fell against the table. It wasn't funny really but he came out with such a mouthful that we all fell about laughing. He's recovered now so we'd better keep out of the way or he might just give up...............

An hour later and we have garlands from corner to corner, in red, green, white and golden yellow throughout the downstairs with the tree looking beautiful, standing on a table in the bay window. We never close the draw curtains over the bay throughout Christmas while the tree is up so it is always in full view. We've just been outside to see how it looks from the road and can't decide if it looks better with the lights on constant or with the flicker bulb in but in any case, we all agree that it's the best tree in the road. With the windows misting up round the edges it looks like something from a Christmas card...............

It's Saturday again now with only four more days to Christmas and no more school for two weeks so I'm not going to give it a thought, not that I give school much thought while I'm there. It's been an exciting week one way or another but it wasn't all good I'm very sorry to say...............

We, that is the five of us, thought it would be funny to put a note through one of our neighbour's doors, telling her the police had called while she was out. We selected Mrs Hurst from round the corner, one of the nicest people you could meet, simply because I had seen the whole family pass our house earlier so assumed the house to be empty. I didn't allow for any of the neighbours seeing us deliver our "Christmas card". Mrs Hurst's next door neighbour did, however, see us all run up and down the path and when Mrs Hurst showed her the scrawled note, we were revealed as the culprits. That didn't go down very well all round as we were in trouble and got a good telling off from a very disappointed mum and dad but then luckily for us, Mrs Hurst, amazingly, seemed to see the funny side and forgave us...............

The estate had an evening visit from Father Christmas in his coach, in all its splendour, to the top of Sefton Close. The coach really was a vision of gold and silver and looked like something out of a fairy tale so it wasn't only the little children who were entranced, everybody was. The outside of the coach was completely covered in fairy lights and it was the most realistic Father Christmas I have ever seen. People were spellbound as we watched him and heard him call out wishing everybody a merry Christmas, to the sound of the Christmas carols playing..............

We also had a visit from Auntie May and Uncle Joe who brought our Christmas present - something for the family to share - like they did last year. We have had some fantastic presents from them over the years. I think I was three the first time I remember a parcel arriving from America from Auntie May, before she was married. She sent something especially chosen for each one of us, which would arrive in a huge cardboard box and that year when I was three, my present was a beautiful dress. Even at the age of three I could see how lovely it was as I called it my American dress. Then when they married, she and Uncle Joe continued with Auntie May's tradition. When they returned home to the UK, they still gave us a lovely present each year until last year when it all changed.

I had walked in from school when mum said Auntie May and Uncle Joe had called during the day to drop off our Christmas box which mum said I'd find in the kitchen. I asked what they had sent and she just told me to go and see, with the twinkle she has in her eyes sometimes. I dashed through to the kitchen to see the treats and sure enough there was one huge cardboard box lying across the top of the stove. The box had been opened and when I looked inside I thought, "Strange, that can't be it", but looking round the kitchen there were no other boxes. I lifted the packing from around the contents to get a better view of our present, singular it seemed. In place of the usual treats of nightdresses, scent or jewellery for the girls, as well as boys' things, was the biggest selection of fruit and nuts I have ever seen outside a shop. If I said I wasn't disappointed I'd be lying as I stood and stared in disbelief at the box. I really did appreciate how kind Auntie May and Uncle Joe had always been and were continuing to be but as I stood there turning over the fruit I wondered why, if they had to send an edible treat, couldn't it have been chocolate?..............

Having all been given extra pocket money to do our Christmas shopping, we are now in Woolworths in the town centre. Monica and Sheila have bought mum a string of "pearls" from here for the past two years but this morning she took them to one side to tell them that the pearls were actually a bit too short for her and she couldn't wear them. We all thought she was saving them for best but not to worry, it'll be nice to find something different.

They have now chosen Yardleys lavender bath cubes and talc in a gift box which mum will love and she will definitely be able to use. I can smell the cubes through the wrapping paper and it's lovely. Margaret and I couldn't agree on what to buy for mum, no surprise there, so I bought some white cotton hankies and we're off to the haberdashery stall on the market to buy some embroidery cotton. I'm going to stitch a petal pattern round all the edges and then write "mum" on one corner. Margaret bought a box of Clarnico Peppermint Creams which are mum's favourite. It's all very exciting this although we're struggling over what to buy for dad. It's always a case of getting him something he needs more than what he likes because it's so difficult. The only things I know he likes are cigarettes and books and I wouldn't know what book to get him because mum says he only likes the ones with blood dripping down the front, so I do believe it's going to be socks and hankies again for dad...............

The walk home took about twelve minutes with John suggesting we played knock and run to pass the time while we were walking. I suggested instead that we walked home in an orderly fashion and try looking like normal people. I despair sometimes, I really do. He disappeared from sight at one point and popped up behind St Chad's church wall to bombard us with snowballs...............

It's bedtime now, still Saturday and I feel a bit bad, a bit guilty, about something else this time. While mum and dad were out shopping again we went looking for our presents and found them in mum's locked wardrobe. I prised the door open for me, Margaret, John, Monica and Sheila to see our presents. I can't see that it was exactly a sin but it was wrong so I'll have to tell it in confession even though it won't make me feel much better I'm sure. I know it wasn't just me but but I'm responsible as I'm the eldest. What's done is done and there's no going back so we've all sworn each other to secrecy.

Our presents used to be kept locked away in the

airing cupboard on the landing until the year before last when Gerry took it upon himself to enlighten Monica and Sheila about the true meaning of Father Christmas, as he unlocked the cupboard, revealing all the presents. I would never have done that and I'm not sure what came over Gerry but think it may have been just that he knew something we didn't and was simply showing off..............

It's now Monday morning. I thought for a minute it was a school day as I was waking up but no, it's Christmas Eve at last, the best day of the year, better than Christmas day, with all the excitement of tomorrow still ahead of us. It is also the busiest day and mum asked for "all hands on deck today" so I'm diving out of bed to ask what needs doing.

I'm the last up and go down to find John and the girls in the kitchen having their breakfast while mum is hard at work already, but enjoying herself, sorting out the Christmas fayre. Mum always makes two Christmas cakes, one for decorating, which is standing on the dresser now in pride of place but still devoid of any icing. The other one we finished off a week ago. There are two huge Christmas puddings which mum steamed, wrapped in cloths and tied with string, for many hours until the steam filled the house. We all had a stir of the puddings, for luck, and mum has put some sixpences in each one.

There's a whole array of other goodies surrounding the cake - we have chocolate biscuits, figs, dates, pickles, blackcurrant cordial as it's Christmas and then of course there is the box of fruit and nuts from Auntie May and Uncle Joe. The cold stuff is kept in the pantry, such as butter, eggs, milk and salad. We also keep the tinned food in the pantry. We have tins of cream, tinned fruit, a huge tin of pilchards for tonight's tea as well as the annual tin of red salmon.

On Christmas Eve we always have pilchard salad which mum calls "the famine before the feast". The feast actually starts after midnight as dad cooks a piece of ham to be served when Julie gets back from midnight mass and the boys come home from their night out, but the feast starts on Christmas morning for the rest of us...............

And so to the itinerary for the day. I ask mum what the plan is and she says she will be baking mince pies, making the trifle and preparing tomorrow's dinner for most of the day so could me and Margaret help with the housework. I'm not sure about Margaret but that suits me fine as I like doing housework, so give us a couple of hours and the whole house will shine. The only problem then will be keeping it like that, just for the day. Julie, Gerry and Eddie are working half day today and dad of course is at work as usual...............

It's six o'clock. The house is shining clean and smells of a mixture of the fire burning in the front room and the boiler burning in the kitchen with the clothes drying in front of both, all mixed together with mince pies and tangerines. Mum has just opened the pilchards so that spoilt the ambience somehow but not to worry - they taste nice at least..............

Old Mother Riley was on television this afternoon but none of us had much of a chance to watch it. The only thing we sat down to watch was Emergency Ward 10 and now it's time for bed. The dishes are washed, the washing dried and ironed and the house is gleaming as we go upstairs. Julie, Gerry and Eddie are out and it's now time to leave mum and dad on their own to relax for a couple of hours with their bottle of Harvey's Bristol Cream sherry, when dad comes down, as he actually disappeared upstairs twenty minutes ago so I guess it's something to do with present wrapping. As we walk into our room though, he's just removing the newspaper from the front of the fireplace and turns to look at us with a huge smile as the fire blazes..............

I stir in my sleep a few hours later and reach up for my sock to find "he's been". I can now smell Christmas from the apple, the hazlenuts and walnuts and especially the tangerine that fill my sock. It's still the middle of the night judging by the pitch black which is all I can see through the curtains, as the street lights are switched off for the night..............

I'm fully awake now and after dashing down the stairs to the front room, the clock shows it's half past six. John had crept into our room to wake us. I had asked him to make sure he did it quietly and to give him his due, you'd have thought it was a military operation the way he tiptoed out, not wanting to wake the others. Then as we are on our way down the stairs, that is me, Margaret, John, Monica and Sheila, he has the biggest smile as he calls out, "For all I know, I might even have a fort". The others don't know about that so we all turn to tell him to shush but I am glad to see that seeing his presents in advance doesn't seem to have spoilt his excitement, quite the reverse in fact. There are still lots of surprises here, bought since the wardrobe break in. There are two dolls, a brown one and a white one sitting in a doll's pram wrapped in yards of paper for Monica. We had actually seen the dolls and guessed they were for Monica but we hadn't seen the pram. Monica has already chosen names for her dolls - Penny and Jenny. There are also new quilted housecoats for each of the girls in pretty pastel shades...............

Before long the room is a sea of wrapping paper with books, bags, a scooter, games and selection boxes. We stack the paper by the fireplace and then between us we clear the grate to light a new coal fire before heading for the kitchen to make a pot of tea to take up to mum and dad on one of the rare occasions when they can both have a lie in...............

We're now off to the early mass at half past eight at Father Ramsbottom's with mum. John will be on the altar and mum has to lecture him on the way, to behave himself. By the time we get home everybody should be up.

We're disappointed not to have had a white Christmas as for the past week all we've had is wind and rain although it is very, very cold and I'll be glad to get back after mass to the warmth and the smell of mince pies and the two turkeys roasting in the oven which mum put in before we left. We need two turkeys to go round us all which mum has names for - Geoffrey and James - the same names every year...............

We're back home now and Gerry has just come down. He was sitting in the armchair with his bare feet sticking out, just looking at us without saying anything. John asked him if he was alright and he said, "Yes, I'm just waiting for my socks."

Eddie is busy examining his new fishing tackle and Julie has a new record player which is good because she keeps her records in the front room and I'll be able to play some of them perhaps, while she is out. She's got the new Elvis record for Christmas but some of her older ones are my favourites, like Running Bear and Tell Laura I love her...............

Dinner is ready now and it's time to close the doors to the world until tomorrow. It's time now to be ourselves with all guards dropped. We're all here together and we can laugh at each other and at ourselves as well as telling funny and interesting stories from the year. We don't dwell on problems today.

After dinner we have one more present to come which is dad's surprise to us. He keeps a silver coloured coach with tiny doors that open to reveal tiny compartments and each year after Christmas dinner he opens the coach doors to give us an extra treat - always just a small thing like a bit of jewellery for the girls or key ring or magnet for the boys - the pleasure is in the opening of the tiny compartments.

We actually have a Christmas tea a few hours after dinner - you wouldn't think you could be hungry again. That's when mum opens the tin of salmon and it's now time for the trifle and mince pies - then following this we collapse in front of the television for the rest of the day. As dad lets the older ones have a drop or two of the sherry, Gerry is on form and making us all laugh again. We'll be watching Christmas Night with the Stars hosted by Eamonn Andrews. Mum's favourites of The Black and White Minstrels and Russ Conway are on tonight as well as Andy Stewart who dad doesn't like. I have no idea why, but dad seems to take exception to people sometimes if they just get on his nerves...............

I'm struggling to stay awake now. Christmas was good though and with a last smile for Christmas I'm about to lie down when I see from the gap in the curtain at the side of the window that it's snowing heavily.

ooooooooooooooo

It did indeed snow again that year as the weather changed on Boxing Day when the snow we had been waiting for came and fell for four days without stopping, causing huge drifts nationwide, Kirkby included. The severe weather conditions also played havoc with transport up and down the country but for us, well, we just made the most of it as the snow turned to ice which was to hang around for weeks, providing us with ice rinks on anything from a puddle, a pond or a frozen lake for the older ones.

I had long since stopped believing in Father Christmas by that time as I was thirteen but I continued to check if my sock was full until the last time dad played Father Christmas when I was nineteen.

Conclusion

If I were to describe our lives as simple, I can just hear dad saying:-

"Simple! I'll give you simple. When did you ever see your mummy sit down to take a rest from it all?"

He wouldn't have considered himself. We all came first.

Other words I could use to describe our lives could be, straightforward; happy; difficult; poor, as well as rich.

As to how mum managed to sing, well, that became obvious as whenever I looked back to see her, dad was never very far away.

I enjoyed my journey back with my brothers and sisters. Some of the memories made us laugh while some were tinged with a little sadness that it's all over now.

Loving Wishes
on
OUR SILVER
WEDDING

315

Only you and I can share
Our Silver Wedding Day,
The memories that it holds for us,
The joy it brings our way...
And there is nothing nicer, dear,
Than knowing you and I
Will go on sharing...caring, too,
As days and years go by!

To Madge

From
Ted xxxxx

Acknowledgements

Thank you to my brothers and sisters for shared memories

Geoffrey Plant - author of The History of Kirkby

Kirkby Teacher Training College Alumni Society - Malaysia

Reverend David Long - supply of old Kirkby photographs

Philippa Hartley - present day photographs

Harry and George.